ACEDIA AND ITS DISCONTENTS

Metaphysical Boredom in an Empire of Desire

✝

R. J. Snell

ACEDIA
AND ITS DISCONTENTS

*Metaphysical Boredom in
an Empire of Desire*

+

 Angelico Press

First published
by Angelico Press 2015
© R. J. Snell 2015

For information, address:
Angelico Press
4709 Briar Knoll Dr.
Kettering, OH 45429
angelicopress.com

978-1-62138-126-6 (pbk)
978-1-62138-127-3 (ebook)

Cover image: Andrey Mironov
Adam and Eve, The Fall of Man, 2012
Cover design: Michael Schrauzer

CONTENTS

For Amy

Catch us the foxes,
the little foxes,
that spoil the vineyards,
for our vineyards are in blossom.

Song of Songs 2:15

Preface

The Empire of Desire

In an essay for *First Things*, R.R. Reno develops Richard Weaver's insight that "every man participating in a culture has three levels of conscious reflection: his specific ideas about things, his general beliefs or convictions, and his metaphysical dream of the world."[1] On the first two levels, Reno suggests, the denizen of the contemporary West lives in a highly regulated world disciplining everything from bike helmets to smoking, local produce to competitive preschool, while remaining thoroughly antinomian in their metaphysical dreams: "We are trained to be suspicious of long-standing moral traditions; we are told to adopt a critical attitude toward inherited norms.... It serves a moral conviction, widespread though often tacit: that human beings flourish to the degree that they're free to satisfy their personal desires."[2] Many feverishly obsess about their kids' athletic and academic accomplishments, stricken with moral shame if they fail to land an internship, but unperturbed at their religious inactivity or sexual activity (so long as they're safe). Such a combination of discipline and laxity is not, one suspects, properly ordered. Or, as Reno criticizes, the "countless little disciplines" enacted "to ensure health, productivity, success, and social harmony" are utilized only to create "space for bespoke lives tailored to our desires."[3]

This Empire of Desire finds limits repugnant. As such, many in the contemporary West are deeply infected with the vice of sloth, with *acedia*, called the "noon day demon" by early desert fathers. Burrowed to the roots of our culture's self-understanding and

---

1. R. R. Reno, "Empire of Desire," *First Things* (June/July 2014): 26.
2. Ibid.
3. Ibid.

metaphysical dreams, sloth is enmeshed in our very way of being, our vision of what it means to be human. We have made a terrible covenant with sloth—we give it our deepest hopes and longings, and in return sloth promises each of us our own Empire of Desire. What the tradition deemed an enslaving vice is transformed into the means of freedom, if we just deliver ourselves over to it.

No one escapes covenanting with the Empire of Desire, for even those of us aware of its presence feel its allure, thrill at its whispers. We cannot live without mirroring the convictions of our place and time, and so we are fragmented. Consequently, this book, then, is for everyone wishing to escape the Empire and immigrate to the Civilization of Love and for anyone with daughters or sons, nieces or nephews, mothers or fathers, goddaughters or godsons, or anyone they love and wish freed from the Empire. It is also, I trust, for all the faithful included in the universal call to holiness and responsible for the new evangelization; if we, and those we love, are to be saints, and if we are to bring good news to a waiting world, then we must know the vice blocking our ears and loves.

In the following pages, I look at sloth in its historical and contemporary meanings and suggest a few, though certainly not all, approaches to rooting it out. No panaceas or programs here, but a form of resistance, a call to reconfigure our imaginations, practices, and metaphysical dreams by returning to a deep appreciation of the wisdom found in the Christian tradition. As I see it, Christians should return to their sources—*ad fontes*—not only out of pious regard for the past but in expectation of vitality, recognizing the ever ancient as ever new, capable of guiding us through feverish times. We return not in arid commitment to what has been merely because it was, but into the liveliness of a heritage. We turn back in order to live well.

I have benefited from presenting these ideas to several audiences from whom I've received helpful suggestions. With that in mind, I owe much to Esther Meek and the Bitar Lectures at Geneva College, the Humanities Faculty at Villanova University and the Faith and Culture Lecture, Jonathan Yonan and the Templeton Honors

Forum, the Lonergan Workshop at Boston College, Mark Gottlieb and the Tikvah Summer Institute, several sections of the Art and Culture course at Eastern University, and John Yates III who hosted me for a writing retreat. John Riess and others at Angelico have been gracious in their improvements, and I'm thankful. Thanks also to my friends, colleagues, and supporters at Eastern University, the Templeton Honors College, and the Agora Institute, especially Phil Cary, Jeff Dill, Kelly Hanlon, Monica Jekel, Steve McGuire, Jocelyn Paul, Fred Putnam, and Amy Richards. Always, too, that little outpost of the Church which is my family.

✝

With gratitude I acknowledge the editors of *The City*, *The Covenant Quarterly*, and the *Lonergan Workshop* for allowing me to use materials previously appearing in their pages, although revised and reconfigured for this text.

"The Gift of Good Sex: Thinking Contraception Anew." *The Covenant Quarterly* 66 (Summer 2008): 24–37.

"Lust to Annihilate: Terrible Covenant of Sloth." *The City* (Winter 2011): 82–93.

"Sloth Transposed: The Friendless Universe." *Lonergan Workshop* 24 (2013): 407–20.

Introduction

A Lust to Annihilate:
The Terrible Covenant of Sloth

I recall no depictions of violence in literature more horrifying than those given by the novelist Cormac McCarthy, now most famous for *No Country for Old Men* and *The Road*. And of all his terrors, I know of none more awful than the depravity unveiled in *Blood Meridian* through the character of Judge Holden, one of the most satanic figures ever concocted.[1] Accurately understood as a type for strife and war, I find the judge guilty also of a vice the Christian tradition labels *acedia*, or sloth. What's most disturbing is how compellingly a character of fiction exposes our current cultural reality. The basic underlying disease of the judge—revolt against the grace of creation—now deeply infects the West. Not just a mythic character of American fiction, the judge, i.e., sloth, tries to embrace us all, seeking to place each of us under his terrible covenant. As we become like him—rejecting the thickness of the created order—our freedom becomes unbearably light and we bleach out the dignity of the real in a fit of violence; we embrace a culture of death.

A Terrible Covenant

In *Blood Meridian, or The Evening Redness in the West*, McCarthy recounts the episodes of John Joel Glanton's nihilistic and overwhelmingly violent gang of bounty-hunters as they slaughter, rape, scalp, maim, and desecrate their way across the Southwest. Just reading the book leaves one feeling assaulted, so relentless are the

---

1. Cormac McCarthy, *Blood Meridian, or The Evening Redness in the West* (New York: Vintage International, 1992). As this work is cited often in this Introduction, hereafter page references will be given in parentheses following the quotation.

depictions of meaningless violence played out in an equally harsh and endless desert. Brutality reigns and hope for salvation is quickly extinguished. "War endures," and any other pattern or order is ground into dust before that "ultimate trade."(248)

Early in the novel, the nameless protagonist, "the kid," running away from his drunken father, a man enraged at the son whose mother "did incubate in her own bosom the creature who would carry her off," finds himself drawn into the revival meeting of a Reverend Green.(3) Any chance for salvation is thwarted, however, by the arrival of an enormous, hairless man proclaiming that the reverend is an illiterate fraud, an atheist, and a known pedophile who sometimes resorts to bestiality. Women faint, men prepare a lynching, and gunfire rings out as the tent collapses, leaving participants "trampled underfoot in the mud."(7) The source of the chaos, "the judge," departs for drinks, cheerfully admitting he has lied, that he knows nothing of Reverend Green, an admission prompting widespread admiration and revelry. The judge appears to have destroyed a religious leader and the community made possible by religion for no other reason than that he could. An act of sheer choice, of pure will.

The breakdown of social control is contagious. The kid gets into several vicious fights, fleeing town—to the smiling delight of the judge—with dying men and a burning hotel in his wake. Thus infected, it is no surprise when the kid joins the gang of Captain Glanton to take Apache scalps for bounty. The gang is without mercy or order, killing randomly anyone they happen to meet. To the kid's surprise, Judge Holden is also a member of the gang, although he seems to have some unique authority or jurisdiction over everyone in the group. Indeed, every man in the gang claims, just like the kid, to have come under the judge's influence prior to joining up with Glanton—an uncanny improbability.

The judge has authority, like some perverse Moses leading his people through the desert. At some point prior to the kid's membership, the gang runs out of gunpowder and helplessly flees from pursuing Apaches, with "no place to run and no place to hide."(125) As they flee, they "come upon the judge on his rock there in that wilderness by his single self."(126) There is only one rock in the wasteland, an oddity causing some in the gang to suspect that "he'd brung it with him...to mark him out of nothing at all." (125) Appearing in the vastness without apparent cause, "you couldn't tell where he'd come from," for he is without horse or canteen, just sitting on this rock "like he'd been expectin us." (125) When Glanton informs him of their situation, Judge Holden takes charge, calmly leading the men "like the disciples of a new faith" to refine their own gunpowder. (130) The Apaches close in, but "it was a butchery," with "that queer powder" bestowing a kind of power: "it was sharp shooting all around and not a misfire in the batch." (134) From that point on, Holden and Glanton have a "secret commerce," a "terrible covenant," confirming the judge's unifying authority. (126) All under Glanton's charge are now covenanted to the judge who lays claim to them all.

Just as his appearance in the desert, the entire history of Judge Holden is strange; in fact, he seems to not have a past so much as to endlessly recur. At one point the gang returns to Chihuahua to receive payment for their trophies of war. As each goes to the public baths to wash away the gory remnants of their exploits, they descend "one by one into the waters...all tattooed, branded, sutured...some deformed, fingers missing, eyes, their foreheads and arms stamped with letters and numbers as if they were articles requiring inventory." (167) Each and every member of the gang bears history in some visible and bodily way—*except* for the judge. Not only is he "strangely childlike" (6) and completely hairless, but as he disrobes to enter the "thin gruel of blood and filth" he reveals no marks at all, no traces of any past reality. (167) His body is bare, pink, baby-like. He seems to belong to no one except himself, bound to no customs, laws, or ways of being other than those he has given to himself. He is judge, never judged.

Judge Holden, though his historical reality is dubious, is portrayed as the most educated man in the territory, with immense erudition and knowledge of geology, geography, natural history, myth and literature, languages, indigenous peoples, and human history. He discourses frequently and eloquently on a variety of subjects and his authority over his interlocutors is absolute. In his notebook he sketches plant and animal life, geological finds, landscapes, and artifacts from early cultures. Oddly, however, he often destroys what he captures in his notebook—after sketching some ancient cave drawings he scratches the originals off the cave wall and out of existence. Similarly, he sketches various pieces of armor and weaponry left centuries before by the Spanish before destroying the artifacts:

> he took up the little footguard and turned it in his hand and studied it again and then he crushed it into a ball of foil and pitched it into the fire. He gathered up the other artifacts and cast them also into the fire ... and he seemed much satisfied with the world, as if his counsel had been sought at its creation. (140)

For the judge, knowledge is a kind of hunt; he captures reality in his notes, attempting to dominate being.

The judge treats all being, personal and impersonal, this way, as something to possess and discard. While the judge had accused Reverend Green of sexual deviancy, Holden is the true pedophile, collecting small children as playthings before murdering them, taking their scalps for trophies and dumping their lifeless bodies to rot in the desert heat. While McCarthy, mercifully only hints at the violations, they occur nonetheless. At another point, the judge makes a pet of a mentally handicapped man, seemingly for no other reason than to best Glanton who had claimed power to tame any animal which eats. The "idiot" had been exploited by his own brother in a kind of circus before being liberated by the judge, who leads him on a leash, feeding him by hand until discarding him as useless human detritus.

Judge Holden explains himself at one point, articulating his reason for capturing and erasing any reality not under his direct control. He had been showing enormous interest in animal and plant life, pressing leaves and plants into his notebook, studying butterflies, shooting and dressing a virtual aviary of mountain birds, until asked his purpose. His response is haunting:

> Whatever exists, he said. Whatever in creation exists without my knowledge exists without my consent. ... These anonymous creatures ... may seem little or nothing in the world. Yet the smallest crumb can devour us. Any smallest thing beneath yon rock out of

men's knowing. Only nature can enslave man and only when the existence of each last entity is routed out and made to stand naked before him will he be properly suzerain of the earth. (198)

Asked the definition of a suzerain, he answers that it is a special kind of ruler, one ruling "even where there are other rulers," one whose authority "countermands" other judgments. (198) The judge's authority is such that no other autonomous life is permitted— "nothing must be permitted to occur . . . save by my dispensation," even if that means killing or molesting everything under his rule. (199) The freedom of birds, for example, "is an insult." (199)

In the very end, the kid resists the judge. Perhaps it was the memory of his drunken father's reading of "poets whose names are now lost," but the kid's early susceptibility to the judge weakens over time. (3) All the other members of the gang appear joined in their "terrible covenant," but the kid alone, despite his atrocities, offers some help and mercy to his fellows, even refusing at one point to murder Holden. The judge knows of the kid's flickering remainder of decency, stating, "I'd have loved you like a son" except "you alone were mutinous. You alone reserved in your soul some corner of clemency." (306, 299) Doing so, the kid loses the judge's permission to kill and maim and violate and becomes guilty. He is a "witness against" himself, claims the judge, for he "sat in judgment on [his] own deeds" and did not give in entirely to the way of war. (307) Holden simply cannot abide this, must reassert his status as suzerain, and murders the kid in an outhouse; "he rose up smiling and gathered him in his arms against his immense and terrible flesh" before proclaiming his ultimate victory—"He says that he will never die." (333–35)

The judge of fiction serves as a diabolical revelation of our actual malaise, one held captive to the madness of sloth. Having rejected any norms given in creation, freedom is under no authority other than the awful lightness of the will; we are free to do as we wish, including violence against all being.

Sloth, Everything a Plaything

Acedia, the "noon day demon," so called since it strikes in the tedium of the afternoon, receives a surprising amount of attention in early monastic literature. Evagrius of Ponticus, a fourth-century Egyptian monk, considers it the most troublesome of the demonic thoughts, describing the demon as follows:

> he causes the monk continuously to look at the windows and forces him to step out of his cell and to gaze at the sun to see how far it still is from the ninth hour, and to look around, here and there, whether any of his brethren is near. Moreover, the demon sends him hatred against the place, against life itself, and against the work of his hands. . . .[2]

Sloth is not laziness, although the term in time does come to mean mere inactivity. Rather it reveals frustration and hate, disgust at place and "life itself." In *acedia*, the monk abhors what God has given, namely, reality and the limits of order, especially the limits of one's own selfhood.

Thomas Aquinas describes sloth as a sad rejection of loving, intimate union with the Creator. Since such union, according to Aquinas, is our ultimate happiness and joy, sloth very oddly rejects happiness and chooses sorrow instead. We are made for God, but sloth hates our *telos*; in fact, the slothful considers our purpose distasteful, even repellent, detesting the personhood God has given. Jean-Charles Nault describes this as a collapse into self:

> *Acedia* . . . is a profound withdrawal into self. Action is no longer perceived as a gift of oneself, as the response to a prior love that calls us, enables our action, and makes it possible. It is seen instead as an uninhibited seeking of personal satisfaction in the fear of "losing" something. The desire to save one's "freedom" at any price reveals, in reality, a deeper enslavement to the "self." There is no longer any room for an abandonment of the self to the other or for the joy of gift; what remains is sadness or bitterness within the one who distances himself from the community and who, being

---

2. Siegfried Wenzel, *The Sin of Sloth: Acedia in Medieval Thought and Literature* (Chapel Hill: University of North Carolina Press, 1967), 5.

separated from others, finds himself likewise separated from God.[3]

It is a mistake to think that sloth is laziness. The slothful might very well be busy doing things. Evagrius claims, in fact, that the slothful are often in a frenzy of pointless action—now this, now that—in their disgust at the actual work given to them by God. We might anticipate the slothful to be very busy and, as the purposelessness of their lives is revealed, increasingly destructive. More than indolence, sloth rejects the burden of order, choosing instead the breezy lightness of freedom. Loving self more than relation, and autonomy more than the good, in sloth one rejects the weight and density of living in an ordered creation.

Addiction to freedom is a revolt of the self against any construction of the world that demands respect or piety, that is "thick" or full enough of meaning to demand our recognition and respect. The weight of reality is viewed as an insufferable demand, as oppression, an illegitimate restriction of freedom. The best remedy against sloth, at least according to Evagrius, is one our freedom would find disgusting, for it requires remaining under the yoke, *hypomonè*. Keeping yoked, that is, maintaining fidelity, is unbearable to the suzerains of the world.

In *Sources of the Self*, Charles Taylor proposes that moral space—the framework by which we orient our lives and values—is essential to personhood. Moral space is "ontologically basic," and without it we could not exist as persons, losing capacity for rational action. But as Taylor writes, "it is now commonplace about the modern world that it has made these frameworks problematic . . . traditional frameworks are discredited or downgraded to the status of personal predilection."[4] Moderns are not so sure about frameworks anymore, as they have all become unhooked from any fixed point. We have become like Judge Holden, free from moral space, as if simply appearing in the desert without history, custom, mores, or sociality.

---

3. Jean-Charles Nault, "Acedia: Enemy of Spiritual Joy," *Communio* 31 (Summer 2004): 245–46.

4. Charles Taylor, *Sources of the Self* (Cambridge: Harvard University Press, 1989), 16.

Modern freedom resulted when older moral horizons were uprooted, when "liberation" from the "captivity" of divine order was attained. Free, yes, but the world seems to have lost its story, and we suffer "a sense of malaise, emptiness."[5] As Taylor explains in *A Secular Age*, our freedom is disembedded from reality, with a resulting "terrible flatness in the everyday," the "utter flatness, emptiness of the ordinary."[6] Our freedom came at a cost: the loss of anything worth living for, and the only remainder is a "centring on the self."[7] And since the world is devoid of thickness, everything becomes a plaything, something to tame, toy with, lead about on a leash, and discard when we have drained its temporary pleasure.

The Freedom of Birds and the Glory of God

A story positing the status of creatures allows us to recognize the value of these things. Not simply the products of world force or chance but of God's loving and reasonable choice, all things are recipients of generosity, receiving themselves as gift. They are graced, and their freedom is borrowed since they cannot maintain their own existence without the sustaining work of God, in whom they live and move and have their being. Dependency does not reduce value but rather grants dignity, a notion fundamentally counter to those for whom the freedom of birds is insulting. God's glory does not diminish ours, and our dignity is not a threat to God, for God's own glory, in part, is us. The glory of God is present to things as the graciousness of their being; things are never just themselves, they carry the weight of God along with them. Things are not light, but unbearably heavy.

A repugnance of order—Judge Holden's *acedia*—demands the violation of things as an act of final emancipation. By refusing to acknowledge the weight of God's glory, things lose density and

5. Charles Taylor, *A Secular Age* (Cambridge: Belknap Press of Harvard University Press, 2007), 302.
6. Ibid., 309.
7. Charles Taylor, *The Ethics of Authenticity* (Cambridge: Harvard University Press, 1991), 4.

become thin, *bleached out*. The freedom of birds insults, and the
height of revolt against God is to scratch them out. Dependence on
God disgusts the slothful, and the weight and dignity given by God
insults the suzerains of the desert.

Moderns are tempted to consider the world as what Heidegger
termed "standing reserve," an undifferentiated set of resources
awaiting our use. Rather than having the status of creatures full of
God's weight, things are just there, standing at attention before our
desires, waiting to be led around on a leash. Things of the world
become objects distanced and alienated from us, problems to overcome with some sort of method or technique. For the medievals, a
thing known—a tree or cat, say—was a *subject* of being, it held its
own act of existence, whereas we view things as objects. As subjects,
creatures had interiority, a form or nature or essence that we did
not create but were nevertheless bound to recognize. Now things
are objects under our judgment, waiting to be captured in a sketch
and cast aside. If we are not bound by the things, but they by us,
what limits our use other than our own will? In what way can our
desires be ordered so as to respect the integrity of things when their
meaning is determined by the awful lightness of our whims?

John Paul II warned repeatedly against an irrational account of
freedom and the violence lurking behind it, teaching that "crimes
against life" would be justified "in the name of the rights of individual freedom."[8] We are not so different from Judge Holden when our
system of enshrined crime

> destroys itself, and becomes a factor leading to the destruction of
> others, when it no longer recognizes and respects *its essential link
> with the truth.* . . . [O]ut of a desire to emancipate itself from all
> forms of tradition and authority . . . the person ends up by no
> longer taking as the sole and indisputable point of reference for his
> own choices the truth about good and evil, but only his subjective
> and changeable opinion or, indeed, his selfish interest and whim.[9]

When misunderstood autonomy governs our life, it is inevitable

8. John Paul II, *Evangelium Vitae. Encyclical Letter The Gospel of Life* (Boston: Pauline Books, 1995), 4.
9. Ibid., 19.

that the dignity of others must be rejected, for everyone else threatens our unchecked sovereignty. This terrible covenant is especially acute given the new power of technology. Not only have we freed ourselves from the bonds and bounds of creation, but we have alienated ourselves from them, declaring them enemy. Not only against the physical world, although that too, but also other persons and ourselves, as everything is bleached out and rendered defenseless against our frightful autonomy. Finding the world as nought, and ourselves as unchecked, we consume ourselves and all other creatures. To be free as we wish requires hatred of being, even hating life itself, just as Evagrius warned. As John Paul II recognized, this "encourages the 'culture of death' creating and consolidating actual 'structures of sin' which go against life. The moral conscience, both individual and social, is today subjected ... to an *extremely serious and mortal danger.*"[10]

Judge Holden insists on his jurisdiction, finding every creature an object of his terrible judgment. Nothing is allowed freedom or integrity, and no creature is acknowledged as worthy because sustained by God's love. In the end, the kid's resistance to the covenant is futile; the judge hunts him, embraces him in a grasp of death, and scratches him out, like so many creatures before.

We live in a time of open revolt against God's law—a time of sloth. Rather than causing delight and comfort, the story God tells of creation is thought repugnant to our autonomy, and we insist that we are suzerains, those rulers countermanding all other laws, even the rule of God. Limits of body, sexuality, death, or life, all are thought obstacles to overcome rather than considered the graciousness of being. At war with God, we scratch out his creation, especially the weak and fragile, fearing that anything outside our control threatens our freedom.

We cannot avoid the culture of death now; it hunts us, asserting its control, seeking our embrace, claiming covenant over all things. Some resist the judge—just a few, it seems—attempting fidelity, guarding clemency in some corner of their souls. And they are being stalked.

10. Ibid., 24.

Part One

The Weighty Gift of Responsibility

1

From the Dirt, for the Dirt

Viewing himself as suzerain of all the earth, Judge Holden experiences the freedom of other things as profoundly threatening, something to be annihilated. Unlike Holden, God delights in making his creatures free. Even more, God gives to one of his creatures—the human person—the work of being like God, not only in the capacity to act freely, but also to love and delight in all good things. Making us like himself, God charges us to work freely, perfecting both the world and ourselves through our labors, for in the self-donation of our work we enrich the world and fulfill ourselves. But those trapped by the terrible covenant of sloth, on the other hand, abhor self-donation. For them, self-gift is experienced as a wrenching loss of themselves.

Since vice and sin are privations of the good, an adequate grasp of sloth requires first understanding the virtue of good work, itself depending on an even more basic question—"What are people for?" Thus, before we turn to sloth, we begin with an inquiry into that which sloth loathes, or a study of what good work looks like. This chapter considers the basic structure of all reality—gift—and the mandate given by God for humans to enrich the world through the self-gift of work, fleshing out an exploration of good work in the next chapter.

Being as Self-Communication

The Trinity changes everything. Unlike Aristotle's god whose perfection demanded the self-enclosed absorption of *thought thinking thought*, God as revealed by Jesus Christ is *love loving love*. As St. Augustine explains, when we are occupied with "the trinity and about knowing God, the only thing we really have to see is what true love is; well in fact, simply what love is."[1] If we "embrace love," we embrace communion, for charity must be loving, must have an object of love, and must love itself loving: "She is not charity if she loves nothing; but if she loves herself, she must love something in order to love herself as charity . . . but unless it loves itself loving something it does not love itself as charity."[2] Charity, then, always involves three—the *lover*, what is *being loved*, and *love*.

From this Augustine draws an analogy to the Triune relationships. The Father, the Son, and the Holy Spirit are all God, but the Father is not the Son nor the Holy Spirit. The Father begets but is not begotten, the Son is begotten but does not beget, the Holy Spirit proceeds but is neither begotten nor begets. In the love analogy, the Father loves, the Son is beloved, and the Spirit is love itself. Or, as Bernard of Clairvaux would have it, if "the Father is he who kisses, the Son he who is kissed, then it cannot be wrong to see in the kiss the Holy Spirit, for he is the imperturbable peace of the Father and the Son, their unshakable bond, their undivided love, their indivisible unity."[3]

Given their grim obsessions, ancient and contemporary pagans reduce love to power, wondering whether the lover is greater because giving while the beloved receives, or whether the lover is bewitched by the beloved and thus powerless. Transcending such limits, Trinitarian thought insists on the equal nature of all three divine persons, undiminished by giving or receiving love. As personal, the Father possesses Himself, eternally giving his very being to the Son who receives it perfectly without taking possession of something no longer the Father's. Neither is the Son diminished by receiving, for the gift received is the Father's very being, and in receiving the Son is consubstantial with the Father—God from

---

1. Augustine, *The Trinity*, trans. Edmund Hill (Brooklyn: New City Press, 1991), 8. 10.

2. Ibid., 8. 12.

3. Bernard of Clairvaux, *Commentary on the Song of Songs*, arranged Darrell Wright (Internet Archive, 2008), https://archive.org/details/St.BernardOnTheSongOfSongs, 8. 2.

God, light from light, true God from true God. The Father gives perfectly; the Son, receiving perfectly, offers perfect love in return; that endless giving and receiving, never diminished, never diminishing, is a spirit shared so perfectly as to proceed as another person, equally God: "there is a whole, the divine Essence, which is the common good of the three subsisting Relations. With respect to this whole, the Three who compose the Trinitarian society are by no means parts, since they are perfectly identical to it. They are three wholes who are the Whole."[4]

Unlike Aristotle's vision of self-absorption, the Christian understanding of being is fundamentally relational. That which exists, to the extent that it exists in itself, "naturally flows over into being as relational, as turned *towards others* by its self-communicating action. *To be* fully is to be *substance-in-relation*."[5] In a Christian metaphysics, the more something possesses itself, the more it turns to others. The Divine Persons, utterly in act and totally self-possessed, thus are most perfectly relational: "the very inner life of God himself, the supreme fullness of what it means to be, is by its very nature *self-communicative Love*, which then subsequently flows over freely in the finite self-communication that is creation."[6]

Since every effect is like its cause, and since all creation is thereby like its Creator, self-communicative love is the purpose of every creature, albeit in distinct and different ways. Aristotle knew that every being seeks its own act and perfection, but we know more, for we realize that perfection is not atomistic or monadic so much as *giving*. That which gives itself flourishes; the greater the being, the more it is itself as it gives. Being is not some abstract or static property but the principle of act; to be is to be in act, and to be is to possess some principle of act and activity.[7] Insofar as something is it has act, an act which seeks *to* act, *to* operate, *to* perform that which it is: "Each thing

4. Jacques Maritain, *The Person and the Common Good*, trans. John J. Fitzgerald (Notre Dame: University of Notre Dame Press, 1966), 57.

5. W. Norris Clarke, *Person and Being*, The Aquinas Lecture, 1993 (Milwaukee: Marquette University Press, 1993), 14.

6. Ibid., 12.

7. Ibid., 8–10.

appears to exist for the sake of its operation; indeed, operation is the ultimate perfection of a thing."[8] And operation gives forth. Like God, finite things self-communicate. Unlike God, finite things are rich *and* poor. Being rich, they operate and have something to give, but as poor they must *become* full. In keeping with the paradox, richness tends to imply a concomitant poverty. A stone, for instance, has very little to give, but gives all that it has simply by existing. An animal is richer, capable of acting in the world through motion, nutrition, and reproduction, but must *do* a lot more to accomplish these ends. Humans, as free persons, are even richer, for "freedom . . . is rooted in the truth about man, and it is ultimately directed toward communion," and yet our experience of communion seems largely to stand in potency.[9] Created more like God than other beings, we are oddly less ourselves, less fully in act, because we have more to do before we have given well.

In one way our poverty is absolute, for we are contingent beings and can never ground or cause ourselves. We are not necessary, and nothingness is a genuine possibility for us. At the same time, and for the same reason, our richness is apparent, for while we need not be, God chose to create us. For the ancients, contingency was a sign of unintelligibility and lack of value; the doctrine of creation, however, reveals a radical dependence on God, for the world in no way creates or sustains its own existence, and neither must God create out of some inner compulsion or logical necessity. The world does not emanate from God; he freely chose to create, and might have chosen otherwise. Rather than decrease the worth of the world, Christians believe this dependence—poverty, if you wish—sustains value. Creation need not be, but it is *because* God chose to make it so, receiving worth as a free gift of God. Things are "*creaturae*, creatures under the 'Great Economy' of God,"[10] meaning that "if the universe is the gift of the person of God, it follows that it is not

8. Thomas Aquinas, *Summa Contra Gentiles*, trans. Vernon Bourke (Notre Dame: University of Notre Dame Press, 1975), 3. 113.

9. John Paul II, *Veritatis Splendor. Encyclical Letter The Splendor of Truth* (Boston: Pauline Books, 1993), 86.

10. Kenneth Schmitz, *Recovery of Wonder* (Montreal & Kingston: McGill-Queen's University Press, 2005), 29.

indifferent to persons and their values . . . the very character and status of things will reflect their giftedness in their radical contingency and the received generosity inherent in them."[11]

Being created does not diminish but establishes the worth of creatures; neither does the freedom and integrity of creatures pose any threat to God. If God's utter transcendence is denied, then God is like us, existing in fundamentally the same way, just with more power, knowledge, and being. Such a god is only *quantitatively* greater, so our action and being could jostle and compete for space and power with his. But if, as classical theism knows, God is not the first being among beings but transcendent, we do not bump into each other for glory or worth or freedom. Consequently, we avoid viewing the glory of God and our own worth as a zero-sum game:

> If it is true . . . that all that exists exists by God and for God, it is equally true, physically speaking, that all that exists is something "in itself" and "for itself." What God creates depends integrally on the creative efficacy, but if this efficacy is not to be in vain it must produce something, . . . it must produce being . . . [with] an onto-logical status of its own. . . . It is not in spite of its ontological dependence that the creature is really something, since if it is something it is so precisely in virtue of this dependence. . . . [I]t is only in God that we have life, movement, and being, but, then, in Him we really have them.[12]

And, *really having* life, movement, and being, we really have act which seeks its own operation, for its own sake, while simultaneously turning toward others in self-donation.

In no way does God subvert or replace the act of his creatures. Instead, God "always governs things in such a way that it is they that really perform their own operations . . . creatures, from the very fact that they are, must be endowed with efficiency."[13] Aquinas goes further. He suggests that if God alone were the immediate cause of everything it "would imply" not God's greatness, but, instead a "lack

---

11. Ibid., 31.
12. Etienne Gilson, *The Spirit of Medieval Philosophy*, trans. A.H.C. Downes (Notre Dame: University of Notre Dame Press, 1991), 130.
13. Ibid., 131.

of power in the Creator: for it is due to the power of the cause, that it bestows active power on its effect."[14] Christianity, or at least in its Catholic fullness, is *"an integral and solidary humanism,"*[15] and "the name for that deep amazement at man's worth and dignity is the Gospel, that is to say: the Good News. It is also called Christianity."[16]

Gifts in the Garden

Given this metaphysics, it should not surprise us when Genesis confirms God's approval of the world's goodness—*Et videt Deus quod esset bonum* (Gen. 1:21).[17] Further, since all reality is relational, we should understand why God indicates that man should not be alone (Gen. 2:18).[18] As interpreted by John Paul II, Adam's solitude has two meanings—one pointing to the relationship between male and female, the other, concerning us here, disclosing human nature itself, something fundamental and basic to the person, distinct even from the relation of the sexes.[19]

Charged with the task of cultivating the ground (Gen 2:15), a responsibility not given to the animals, Adam's work renders him unique.[20] Still, at this point all the dramatic action is performed by

14. Thomas Aquinas, *Summa Theologica*, trans. Fathers of the English Dominican Province (Notre Dame: Christian Classics, 1981), I. 105. 5 (hereafter *ST*); cf. *Catechism of the Catholic Church*, 2nd ed. (Washington, DC: United States Catholic Conference, 1997), sec. 306: "This use is not a sign of weakness, but rather a token of almighty God's greatness and goodness."

15. Pontifical Council for Justice and Peace, *Compendium of Social Doctrine* (Washington, DC: USCCB Publishing, 2004), 19.

16. John Paul II, *Redemptor Hominis. Encyclical Letter The Redeemer of Man* (Boston: Pauline Books, 1979), 10.

17. All Scripture references will use the Revised Standard Version. *The New Oxford Annotated Bible* (New York: Oxford University Press, 1977).

18. See John Paul II, *Man and Woman He Created Them: A Theology of the Body*, trans. Michael Waldstein (Boston: Pauline Books, 2006).

19. Ibid., 147–48.

20. *Catechism of the Catholic Church*, sec. 307, 308: "To human beings God even gives the power of freely sharing in his providence by entrusting them with the responsibility of 'subduing' the earth and having dominion over it. God thus enables men to be intelligent and free causes in order to complete the work of creation, to perfect its harmony. . . . The truth that God is at work in all the actions of

God. It is God who forms the man, places him in the garden, breathes life into him, and proclaims his aloneness as not good. But if Adam's worth is to be personalized and not merely a higher rung in the chain of being, then his subjectivity must be drawn out from the mere dirt which he is—he must become the subject of action in addition to receiving God's acts.

Nature needs the intervention of God to breathe life into Adam (Gen 2:7) and declare him in God's own image (Gen 1:27). Yet however powerful these symbols, and however true, persons can never be known *as* persons from the cosmological point of view alone but must be experienced from an internal or first person point of view. It is not enough to survey persons objectively; they must rather be considered as subjects who act and are responsible for that action.[21] If Adam is to know his own value, he must know this value not only "objectively" but personally, and so he must experience and know himself as a subject of responsibility. As knowledge cannot be imparted externally, Adam's appropriation of subjectivity cannot be revealed to him by another. Still, Adam needs to be taught, it would seem, and so requires God's instruction.[22] God must bring Adam into his own subjectivity and Adam must experience that subjectivity *as* a subject. But how to accomplish such a thing?

God's solution is a test, an "examination that man undergoes before God (and, in some way, also before himself). Through this 'test,' man gains the consciousness of his own superiority," or comes to encounter himself as a subject.[23] God knows that it is not good for Adam to be alone, but *Adam* must recognize the meaning of his solitude and his need to self-communicate. The instruction is

his creatures is inseparable from faith in God the Creator. God is the first cause who operates in and through secondary causes. . . . Far from diminishing the creature's dignity, this truth enhances it."

21. The acting person is the topic of much of John Paul II/Karol Wojtyla's philosophical work. See R. J. Snell, *The Perspective of Love: Natural Law in a New Mode* (Eugene: Pickwick Publications, 2014), 73–83.

22. The theme of God's instruction in Genesis is explored in the magnificent commentary by Leon R. Kass, *The Beginning of Wisdom: Reading Genesis* (Chicago: University of Chicago Press, 2006).

23. John Paul II, *Theology of the Body*, 148.

gradual, indirect, beginning when God presents the beasts to Adam "to see what he would call them" (Gen 2:19), which the man does, although no fit helper is found among them (Gen 2:20).

Undoubtedly this test prepares Adam for the creation and acceptance of Eve, but "it also has its own deep meaning independently of this creation," for in viewing and naming animals "*the created man* finds himself from the first moment of his existence *before God* in search of his own being . . . in search of his own definition."[24] Man discovers that he is not like the beasts, that he cannot "identify himself essentially with the visible world of the other living beings," and that he is alone.[25] Beyond this negative awareness, man gains also the positive realization of his power to name and distinguish: "*man at the same time reveals himself to himself in all the distinctiveness of his being.*"[26] His solitude is his subjectivity, and he is revealed as personal, with the subjectivity proper to a person.

For John Paul II, the original solitude which Adam begins to understand is marked by self-consciousness—a recognition of himself as a *self*—and self-determination—a recognition of his free responsibility. That is, the ontology proper to the human, one objectively true, is also understood and appropriated by Adam; he not only grasps the concept of "rational animal," but experiences, from within, his own solitude. In his solitude, he alone of all the earthly creation is capable of a unique relationship with God; he is in the very image of a God who is personal and self-communicative, and so can give of himself in a similar way. Only he can do this, unlike the animals, and he can only do this for himself; no one else can do it for him.

While admittedly fanciful, I imagine the test as something like a parade of the animals before Adam. As each animal is found unfit as a helper, Adam's awareness of the situation, and his desire for a helper, develops. Adam grows a bit impatient, looking down the

---

24. Ibid., 149.
25. Ibid. For a fascinating account with many parallels, see the work of Rabbi Joseph B. Soloveitchik, *The Lonely Man of Faith* (New York: Three Leaves Press, 1965).
26. Ibid., 150.

long line with anticipation. "Which one of these will be right? Will any be right?" Eventually, as the last animals are rejected, perhaps dejection and a sense of aloneness. "Is there none right for me? Am I right for any?"

The text provides no such explicit narrative, yet the existential drama present in the text should not be glossed over. In having Adam examine the animals, God is simultaneously having Adam examine himself in order to come to terms with his nature as an acting person. And he is to realize that he is alone, but not meant to be so. Such a realization is jolting, a burst of existential consciousness of who he is and what for. On his own, Adam cannot discover and bring this self into reality. Not only does he need God to instruct him through the "test" of naming the animals, but he cannot create communion for himself. For that to happen, God must act. Adam is fast asleep (Gen 2:21) when God makes Eve, presenting her to Adam as a gift (Gen 2:22). But, however little Adam can do to create or sustain another like himself, he has discovered his own solitude—he knows himself to be embodied as self-conscious and self-determining, a person capable of acting—and for the first time someone other than God speaks (even the naming the animals is reported in the abstract, with no record of what Adam says). Adam acts and speaks for himself (at last) in crying out his joyous acceptance of Eve: "Then the man said, 'This at last is bone of my bones and flesh of my flesh; she shall be called Woman, because she was taken out of Man'" (Gen 2:23). Adam, matured by God's instruction, now acts for himself.

And it is an action, not a mechanical utterance. Adam need not accept Eve. He is aware of his aloneness, even aware that this is not good (or at least that he wants another). "At last," he says, the wait is over, another like me, "bone of my bones and flesh of my flesh." There is another solitude, another self, another person. Still, the instructed Adam, now grasping his own self-determinative freedom, could reject Eve, perhaps returning to some truncated relationship with the animals or, like Narcissus, enacting a life of solitary regard. He could fail the test even as the examination allows his appropriation of selfhood. In rejecting Eve, he would deny the self-communicative perfection of his own being and body, just as he would simultaneously deny the gift that God has brought to him. As such, he would refuse to actualize his covenantal nature and relate improperly to God and himself. For Adam to say no to Eve is to say no to God and to his own nature, even if it would remain a kind of self-mastery "which exalts the isolated individual in an absolute way, and gives no place to solidarity, to openness to others and service of them."[27]

In welcoming Eve, Adam welcomes God and his own fulfillment, choosing self-communication—his operation. Affirming her is "an overcoming of the frontier of solitude and at the same time . . . an affirmation . . . of everything in solitude that constitutes 'man.'"[28] He loses nothing, but gains his own soul when giving of his solitude, when he "opens himself toward a being akin to himself."[29] He is made for *communio personarum*, he exists as a person *for* others, and "*became the image of God not only through his own humanity, but also through the communion of persons.*"[30] That is, the human, while always the image of God, is more fully that image in communion, for then is the divine communion mirrored.

Creation is best read through the hermeneutics of the gift. God creates for no other reason than love, and from that love God "*gives rise to the good and is well pleased with the good*" which is created; as such, creation "signifies *gift*, a fundamental and 'radical' gift, that is, an act of giving in which the gift comes into being precisely from nothing."[31] Precisely because created and not necessary, all creation is a gift. The human, bearing the image of God through no merit or logical necessity, is able to grasp the meaning of gift and to be a gift herself. Persons are God's gift to a gifted world, an elevation and ennobling of what was already good into that which bears the divine image and, in time, will hold the Divine Image's incarnation.

With respect to the man and woman, God's image-bearers stand before each other as gifts-in-themselves and as gifts-for-each other.

27. John Paul II, *Evangelium Vitae*, 19; cf. *Veritatis Splendor*, 31–32.
28. John Paul II, *Theology of the Body*, 162.
29. Ibid.
30. Ibid., 163.
31. Ibid., 179–80.

Instructed and aware of their own status as persons, and delightedly accepting the other as gift, they are free from shame, *"free with the very freedom of the gift."*[32] "At last," Adam says, one like me, bone of bone and flesh of flesh. Another solitude, another person willed for her own sake by a God who gives her to herself and to me. God perfects his creation by calling it good, while Adam's reception of Eve perfects them both (Gen 4:1). If we are actualized in self-communication, if the divine image is most fully realized in mutual gift, then Adam becomes fully alive when he gives himself to Eve *and* accepts her gift to him, just as she becomes fully alive when he accepts her gift of self and she his. We are rich and we are poor, and we attain our perfection when we give and receive gift: *"precisely that love in which the human person becomes a gift* and—through this gift—fulfills the very meaning of his being and existence."[33] Only as each are willed by the other for their own sake, and as each gives to the other, can humans become themselves.

The fundamental structure of the world is gift, or self-communicative love, and the nature of our existence is to act—to operate, rather than simply to exist. To be is to act, to operate for self-donation. But I earlier suggested that *work* played some role in our perfection and end. For that to cohere we need to conduct an initial, somewhat rough analysis of work under the aspect of the gift: approached from within the hermeneutic of the gift, what is work?[34]

The Gift of Work

All too often work is considered a curse, which it is not. In Scripture work is given to humans even before the fall, and although one result of sin is work's disorder, it is not itself a curse. As John Paul II explains in *Laborem Exercens*, "Man is made to be in the visible universe an image and likeness of God himself, and he is placed in it in order to subdue the earth. From the beginning therefore he is *called*

32. Ibid., 185.
33. Ibid., 185–86.
34. I am grateful for a lecture given by D.C. Schindler at Villanova University which helped clarify my thought on this connection.

to work. Work is one of the characteristics that distinguish man from the rest of creatures...."[35] As a peculiar function of the human, present from the very beginning, the task of "making life more human" through work "acquires fundamental and decisive importance."[36] So vital, in fact, that work is central to God's original instruction of the human, telling them already in the first creation account to "fill the earth and subdue it; and have dominion over the fish of the sea and over the birds of the air and over every living thing that moves upon the earth" (Gen 1:28). Activity is necessary, showing that "Man is the image of God partly through the mandate received from his Creator to subdue, to dominate the earth. In carrying out this mandate, man, every human being, reflects the very action of the Creator of the universe."[37]

At times, this mandate of dominion is viewed as supporting a "culture of exploitation," read this way by critics and supporters of such a culture alike.[38] But if the mandate reflects the character of God, and God is fundamentally self-communicative love, then the mandate to subdue the world would best be read as a vocation of self-donation, even if suggesting human mastery. Reducing the analysis to exploitation severs the mandate from the whole purpose of work, something *Laborem Exercens* is careful to avoid.

As a transitive activity, work goes beyond the worker toward the external world, and "thus emerges the meaning of *work in an objective sense,*" as in the domestication of animals, agriculture, technology, and so forth.[39] Still, the *subject* of work is the human, and the mandate of dominion is as much about the human who "manifests himself and confirms himself *as the one who 'dominates'.* This dominion, in a certain sense, refers to the subjective dimension

35. John Paul II, *Laborem Exercens. Encyclical Letter On Human Work* (Vatican Website, 1981), http://www.vatican.va/holy_father/john_paul_ii/encyclicals/docum ents/hf_jp-ii_enc_14091981_laborem-exercens_en.html.

36. Ibid., 3.

37. Ibid., 4.

38. Joseph Ratzinger, *'In the Beginning...' A Catholic Understanding of the Story of Creation and the Fall,* trans. Boniface Ramsey, O.P. (Grand Rapids: Eerdmans, 1995), 33; cf. *Catechism of the Catholic Church,* sec. 373.

39. John Paul II, *Laborem Exercens,* 5.

even more than to the objective one. . . ."[40] As God tested Adam in finding a helper to instruct him into self-understanding from "within," so also the work mandate instructs humans in the meaning of their own subjectivity:

> Man has to subdue the earth and dominate it, because as the "image of God" he is a person, that is to say, a subjective being capable of acting in a planned and rational way, capable of deciding about himself, and with a tendency to self-realization. As *a person, man is therefore the subject of work.* As a person he works, he performs various actions belonging to the work process; independently of their objective content, these actions must all serve to realize his humanity, to fulfil the calling to be a person that is his by reason of his very humanity.[41]

While many may agree that work serves to fulfill the calling of persons, the subjectivism of our time leaves this largely undefined. Not so with John Paul II, for whom communion is the origin, end, and norm of human action, citing *Guadium et Spes* to emphasize that the "root reason for human dignity lies in man's call to communion with God. From the very circumstance of his origin man is already invited to converse with God."[42]

Work is given to us by God as instruction in our own personhood and its demand for self-constitution and governance, including the ability to give; in the end, the purpose of work is *not* the objective goods it brings, however beneficial, for "it is always man who is *the purpose of work.* . . ."[43] Whatever some of the ancient pagans thought, work, including physical work, does not degrade, nor does the toil accompanying work after the fall destroy the dignity of work. Work, or at least good work, is "something worthy;" it "expresses this dignity and increases it," subduing both nature and ourselves. Through it we become "more a human being."[44] The

40. Ibid., 6.

41. Ibid.

42. Second Vatican Ecumenical Council, "Pastoral Constitution on the Church in the Modern World. *Guadium et Spes*" (Vatican, 1965), http://www.vatican.va/archive/hist_councils/ii_vatican_council/documents/vat--et-spes_en.html, 19.

43. John Paul II, *Laborem Exercens*, 6.

44. Ibid., 9.

school of work is also the *gospel of work*, for by work we share in the activity of the Creator and bear a likeness to God, and through it God helps us to realize our personhood and self-donation.[45]

From the Dirt, for the Dirt

At this point, we've seen (1) that all being seeks its own perfection by operating, communicating itself in relation, (2) that Scripture's anthropology reveals humans as created in God's image, thus possessing the solitude of self as a gift perfected by giving itself, and (3) that the task of work is a blessing, a form of instruction allowing us to discover and perfect our subjectivity even as it transforms the objective world. Of course, the quality of work matters, and the next chapter attempts to articulate criteria of good work. Before turning to that task, however, we need to expand a bit on the responsibility of work, again starting with Genesis.

The language of Genesis is compact, rich, and worth noting carefully. For instance, there is an interesting play on the task given to the man (*adam*) who is formed to work the ground (*adamah*):

> one of the linguistic ironies of the Hebrew language is found in the couplet *man/ground*. Even though the man was taken from the dust of the ground in history, etymologically, *adamah* is taken from its root, *adam*. We can infer from this that the ground (and, correspondingly, the earth) was made for and in terms of the man and not vice versa, at least not conceptually.[46]

The earth seems to have a disposition for the man, an aptness or readiness to become personal, as if the earth could somehow "hold" the human. Even the order of creation in the first account seems to build up to man, providing all those things necessary for nature, in Adam, to become conscious, free, and personal: "In man, nature speaks."[47]

45. Ibid., 25.

46. David Bruce Hegeman, *Plowing in Hope: Toward a Biblical Theology of Culture* (Moscow, ID: Canon Press, 2007), 42.

47. Nicholas Wolterstorff, *Art in Action: Toward a Christian Aesthetic* (Grand Rapids: Eerdmans, 1980), 72.

It is entirely proper for the person to be embodied. Catholicism rejects Gnostic disparaging of matter and refuses Cartesian sundering of body from soul. There is no body-self dualism in Catholicism; we are an ensouled body, a hylomorphic union, a body with a spiritual principle and act. We are not souls only, and we await the resurrection of the body rather than the immortality of the soul: "And the LORD God formed the man [*adam*] of the dust of the ground [*adamah*]" (Gen 2:7). We are *from* dirt, and in us the dirt becomes personal. (This same dirt becomes God incarnate, also the body and blood of Christ on the Eucharistic table.)

We are also *for* the dirt. As there is the play between *adam/adamah*, so also between *ish* (man) and *ishshah* (woman), note the "added *He* ('h') at the end of each" pair—*ish* and *ishsh-ah*, *adam* and *adam-ah*.[48] So striking is this parallel that some conclude the text is trying to teach us a profound point about husbandry, in the old sense of care for the soil and animals: "Just as the *ish* is the husband of the *ishshah*, so the man (*ha-adam*) is the husband of the ground (*adamah*). . . ."[49] As the husband of the soil, there is close relationship between our identity and our working the earth, so close that both "man (*adam*) and the earth (*adamah*) . . . have for their root *adom*—'to be red.'"[50] This interplay "between the ruddy man and the red ground/earth is expressed repeatedly in the opening chapters of Genesis," as in the statement "and there was no man [*adam*] to till the ground [*adamah*]" (Gen 2:5).[51]

Now just precisely what it means to be *for* the earth is explored in the next chapter, but for now it suffices to suggest that we bear responsibility. God blesses us with a task of responsibility, to fill, govern, tend, and keep the earth from which we are made (Gen 1:28, 2:15). No other creature bears this weight; certainly our awareness of the task as an obligation and test of our selfhood appears unique, for no other animal loses sleep agonizing over their purpose on earth. We, who are of the very stuff of the soil, carry a responsibility

48. Hegeman, *Plowing in Hope*, 43.
49. Ibid.
50. Ibid., 46.
51. Ibid.

31

the soil does not, and this responsibility is conveyed to us in the mandate to work that same soil. God instructs us, and the divine pedagogy draws out from us, through our labor, our perfection as self-communicating operation (the subjective dimension), even as it contributes to the making of culture and transformation of the earth itself (the objective dimension).

Given his nature, God always seeks to communicate and instruct us in keeping with our freedom and agency. Because he is effusive in his goodness, almost profligate, his instruction furthers every legitimate domain of human well-being and accomplishment. His is not a stingy gift—"Thou openest thy hand" (Ps 145:16)—nor does he disdain those aspects of human life not explicitly religious. Jesus had an ordinary human life as a son, craftsman, and friend, recall, and this was neither below his dignity nor unrelated to his divine vocation, even if it was natural and human:

> Thus, far from thinking that works produced by man's own talent and energy are in opposition to God's power, and that the rational creature exists as a kind of rival to the Creator, Christians are convinced that the triumphs of the human race are a sign of God's grace and the flowering of His own mysterious design.[52]

Dirt Lovers

Fully present only at the end of time, even now we are able to live in such a way that foreshadows, prepares, and embodies a real, if incomplete, likeness to that glory whenever we love well. Such love takes a variety of forms, of course, for *caritas* is fecund, enlivening all that lives and moves and has being; it shines in all that's fair. In its most fundamental form, however, love "signifies much the same as approval. This is first of all to be taken in the literal sense of the word's root: loving someone or something means finding him or it *probus*, the Latin word for 'good.' It is a way of turning to him or it and saying, 'It's good that you exist; it's good that you are in this world.'"[53]

---

52. *Guadium et Spes*, 34.
53. Joseph Pieper, *Faith, Hope, Love* (San Francisco: Ignatius, 1991), 163–64.

Such an expression need not be uttered, but common to all forms of love is the will affirming "I want you (or it) to exist!"[54] Accustomed as we are to considering will from the perspective of practical reason's capacity to bring things about, it may surprise us to think of *willing* that which already is. Clearly, we do not make it so by willing in this way, as it already is. Since God can make things come from nothing merely by willing it so, his will is genuinely productive. But God's love also acknowledges the goodness of existence even if all exists only by his will. Consider the remarkable fact that God not only creates but sustains the world. Since the existence of *everything* at *every moment* depends upon God's eternal and unchanging will to "Let it be! *Esse!*," then all that is, even just now, exists because God affirms that it is good for it to be. *Et Deus vidit quod esset bonum. Et factum est ita.* And it was so, and God saw that it was good.

The teaching of Genesis 2 moves Adam into a position of loving Eve in this basic way, responding to her presence with recognition and affirmation—"At last!"—seeing Eve as God sees her, as good. God saw that she was good—will Adam? He does, and so they stand before each other in mutual regard, without shame, without fear, and without concupiscence. Original nakedness and original unity, as the great pope explained, are not properly understood as a lack of shame, but rather as the full presence of communication and affirmation. Each, fully aware to themselves, gave fully to the other, aware that the other would fully receive that gift—this is more than being unashamed, this is something like the inner life of God.[55] It is to see the other, and the world as well, the way that God sees—*et Deus vidit quod esset bonum.* It is to see it as good, to *approve*, to will (recognize) *goodness*. Consider God's willing of us, as explained by Pieper:

> Many times Jerome puts it that God "wills" man (Ps 18:19), "The Lord has brought me forth into a broad place. He delivered me because he willed me." "*Quoniam voluit me.*" This is quite legitimately rendered in the translation... "Because he loves me." Martin Buber in his translation... also plays upon the erotic

54. Ibid., 164.
55. John Paul II, *Theology of the Body*, 174.

meaning of love, "He has fetched me out into the broad places; he unlaces me, for he has pleasure in me."[56]

He unlaces me, for he has pleasure in me. He wills me. He wills all things as good. Should we do less?

I am suggesting that just as God instructs Adam to *will* Eve in Genesis 2, to recognize and delight in her goodness, so the blessing of work, primarily in its subjective but also in its objective dimensions, is an education in the very same will. In giving us work, God is asking us to *love* the world, and we are *less* like God if we hold back our approval of the world and all that is in it, including our own dynamic agency. Not willing the things of the world, as Pieper means will, is ungodly, diabolical. And work is how we will.

The instruction of Genesis helps us understand that we are responsible to love all that is good, and while we first receive the good things of the world as gift, reception is an active decision to let things be for us, to let them give themselves to us. Is this not what Adam does with Eve? She stands in front of him, and of herself she speaks; from the interior mysteries of her own subjectivity she gives herself as what she is, a self, and he lets her be, he wills her—"At last"—and sees that she is good. He actively receives her riches, unlacing her.

We are also rich. Not only do we have a self to give, but our self is perfected by activity, even if we need to come to learn this through our work. Work is *for us*, helping us to actualize our subjectivity. But this is not an enclosed circle; our work also enriches the world from the springs of our own interior riches, just as Adam is enriched by his acceptance of the riches offered him by Eve. In subduing the garden *we fill it*; our labor does not detract from Eden, but fills it, affirming that we are *for* the dirt. Just the fact of our existence enriches the dirt, for in us the dirt becomes fuller than it was before: more perfect, more like God. And labor contributes even more, for as part of nature *our* elevation elevates *it*, humanizing and materializing our personhood.

56. Pieper, *Faith, Hope, Love*, 165–66.

Conclusion

Father Martin Rhonheimer explains why passion *for* the world is essential to the Gospel:

> God . . . created this world out of love in order to hand it over to the men and women whom he had created in his own image, to complete by their activity and labor the work that the Creator himself had said was "very good." It is a passion that springs from belief in that God who, after man turned away from his Creator and was unfaithful to his original vocation, became man himself in order to save man by giving us his own life and to appoint man as a collaborator in this work of salvation. . . . The world is the real place and workplace of man and woman; it is their task, to which, in both the order of creation and the order of redemption, God has destined his beloved daughters and sons.[57]

As willed by God in creation, every domain of legitimate human work is redeemable and potentially serves, in its own way, to instantiate the love of God. Workers become co-redeemers of themselves (subjective) and the structures of the world (objective).

The original vocation to enrich Eden through our dominion, and in so doing to attain our own end as well, is not vacated by sin; instead, the redeeming work of God, fully revealed as God in Christ, a worker, makes it possible for all thing to be redeemed in their own integrity. If work is to be redemptive, the nature of good work requires explanation.

57. Martin Rhonheimer, *Changing the World: The Timeliness of Opus Dei* (New York: Scepter, 2012), 1–2.

2

The Great Economy:
Three Tests of Good Work

"Work is a particular form of conversation," claims Father Józef Tischner, erstwhile chaplain for Solidarity in Poland, noting the self-communicative aspect of work.[1] The "inner wisdom" of work serves communion "when it sustains life and guarantees its development (the work of a farmer, a physician, a house builder, etc.) or gives a deeper meaning to life (for example, the work of an artist, a philosopher, a priest)" and thereby "acquires its own value and dignity."[2] Not all work gives life, and toil which brings death or exploits life is "sick work or simply not work at all."[3] How are we to tell the difference?

Good work enriches our own subjectivity as it contributes to the bettering of the objective world, while bad work sickens the world and ourselves, perverting our lives. Distinguishing good work from bad, then, would seem a matter of some importance, particularly if sloth's infection impairs our discernment. Fleshing out themes already introduced, this chapter expands on the comprehensive mandates of work given in Genesis before explaining three tests of good work.

The Comprehensive Mandate of Work

In the beginning, we are told, the earth was "without form and void" (Gen 1:2). Filling these lacunae, God creates both structure

---

1. Józef Tischner, *The Spirit of Solidarity*, trans. Marek B. Zaleski and Benjamin Fiore (New York: Harper and Row, 1984), 14–16, 98.
2. Ibid., 15–16.
3. Ibid., 16.

and content, as indicated by the careful ordering of creation. The first day overcomes an absence of form with the creation of light, whereas the fourth day overcomes the absence of content with the creation of the lights—the sun, moon, and stars. Waters are separated from waters on the second day, corresponding with the filling of the heavens and waters with birds and fish on day five. Dry land and its vegetative cover are given on the third day, just in time for the beasts and livestock dependent on them, as well as the humans made from the earth, to fill the land on the sixth day. God builds and fills.

In many ancient Near Eastern accounts, creation motifs "entail a binary *process*: (1) of design, gathering materials and workers, construction, and completion; and (2) of filling the house with fitting contents and provisioning it."[4] The ordinary task of erecting a structure and the larger work of organizing a cosmos require this dual labor, for both structure and content are needed when making a home, or at least doing so with wisdom. In particular, kings are seen to "demonstrate their wisdom by building (big) houses and providing for them," giving a human image by which to understand the divine kingship of God.[5] Like any wise king, God builds himself a palace, albeit on a very grand scale, building the "rooms" in the first three days before provisioning each.[6]

The dual work of building and filling is further emphasized by the distinct types of knowledge or capacity ascribed to each. For instance, building is often described as *wisdom*, expressed in the architectural language of knowledgeable measure and establishment: "The LORD by *wisdom* founded the earth; by *understanding* he *established* the heavens; by his *knowledge* the deeps broke forth, and the clouds drop down the dew" (Pr 3:19–20), or "By *wisdom* a house is *built*, and by *understanding* it is *established*; by *knowledge* the rooms are *filled* with all precious and pleasant riches" (Pr 24:3–

---

4. Raymond C. Van Leeuwen, "Cosmos, Temple, House: Building and Wisdom in Mesopotamia and Israel" in *From the Foundations to the Crenellations: Essays on Temple Building in the Ancient Near East and Hebrew Bible*, ed. Mark J. Boda and Jamie Novotny (Münster: Ugarit-Verlag, 2010), 400.

5. Ibid., 405.

6. Ibid., 408.

4).[7] Houses are built (established) by wisdom—"Wisdom builds her house" (Pr 14:1 and 9:1)—but filled by knowledge. Construction of both the tabernacle and temple of Hebrew Scripture reflect this as well: Bezalel is given wisdom and knowledge in constructing the tabernacle (Ex 31:3), and God fills Hiram with the wisdom, skill, and knowledge (1 Kgs 7:14) needed to build the temple.[8]

God, a wise and cosmic king, establishes the cosmos by wisdom (days 1–3), and fills it by knowledge (days 4–6); the cosmos is his palace. In addition, it appears as though the provision, or filling of the rooms, is an ongoing task completed through the agency of humans. Rather than directly create all that would be, God grants humans the task of filling his temple. Work, then, is the cooperative activity of humans participating with God. The so-called creation mandates of Genesis 1:28 and 2:15 give strong indication of this, for God places humans in the garden to *work* and *keep*, to *govern*, and to *fill*.[9]

This divinely sanctioned pattern of working, keeping, governing, and filling presents a fascinating interplay, especially evident in the relation between keeping and the other mandates. There is no indication that God intended humans to keep the garden in its original condition without effecting any change whatsoever, like a servant charged to meticulously maintain the owner's vision. Not only were

7. Ibid., 409–410.
8. The RSV uses "intelligence" and "understanding" in these passages, although Van Leeuwen explains that the terms and their ordering are strictly parallel in all these texts.
9. The language of Creation Mandates, and a robust reflection on them, is common among the Dutch Reformed tradition, especially in the legacy of Abraham Kuyper. See his *Lectures on Calvinism* (Grand Rapids: Eerdmans, 1931); cf. Richard J. Mouw, *When the Kings Come Marching In: Isaiah and the New Jerusalem*, Revised Edition (Grand Rapids: Eerdmans, 2002); Andy Crouch, *Culture Making: Recovering our Creative Calling* (Downers Grove: IVP Books, 2008); Cornelius Plantinga, *Engaging God's World: A Christian Vision of Faith, Learning, and Living* (Grand Rapids: Eerdmans, 2002); Albert Wolters, *Creation Regained: Biblical Basics for a Reformational Worldview* (Grand Rapids: Eerdmans, 1985). With Fr. Rhonheimer, I think this tradition partially recovers the goodness of ordinary life lost by certain late medieval excesses, and thus worth engaging, but insufficient in its understanding of the Church, sacraments, salvation, and the nature of co-redemption; see *Changing the World*.

the humans told to fill the garden, quite clearly a developmental pattern, but their task of governing and working gives them responsibility for and over the garden. They are not the garden's hired help, but its governors.

Further, this transformational and developmental responsibility is hardly vitiated but rather intensified by the Fall. Quite obviously, sin disrupts and deranges human work, rendering it difficult and, often, fruitless, sometimes even destructive to both the earth and the workers. God retains a place for the products of human work in His vision of redemption, as evidenced by Isaiah 60 where "many of the people and objects from Isaiah's own day appear within [New Jerusalem's] walls, but they have assumed different roles, they perform new functions."[10] Rather than rejecting the results of human work and culture, God seems to welcome them, now transformed and redeemed, into his vision of final peace and righteousness. He even receives the works of idolatrous nations outside of the covenantal community, such as the riches of the "ships of Tarshish" (Is 60:9), the camels, sheep, flocks, rams, gold, and frankincense of Midian, Ephaph, Kedar, Nebaioth which "shall come up with acceptance on my altar," and with which "[God] shall beautify [His] beautiful house" (Is 60:6–7). So too will the trees of Lebanon be used to make the sanctuary beautiful (Is 60:13). God will not annihilate human works, even those done in sin, but will rather transform them, which "gives human work special significance since it bestows independent value on the results of work as 'building materials' of the glorified world."[11] God fills his temple with our work, the garden of Genesis is transformed into the garden-city of Revelation, and much of what fills that city is the redeemed work of our hands.[12]

We are to fill, but also to *keep* the garden—how? As explained by Rabbi Aharon Lichtenstein, Genesis 2:15 provides two distinct tasks, *cultivation* and *guarding* (*tilling* and *keeping*):

10. Mouw, *When the Kings Come Marching In*, 7. In this section, I use the Scripture as Mouw cites it, which differs from the RSV.

11. Miroslav Volf, *Work in the Spirit: Toward a Theology of Work* (Eugene: Wipf and Stock, 1991), 96.

12. Ibid., 9, 98–102; Plantinga, *Engaging God's World*, 103–117; Mouw, *When the Kings Come Marching In*, 17–42.

One, *"le-shomrah"* [guarding/keeping], is largely conservative, aimed at preserving nature. It means to guard the world, to watch it—and watching is essentially a static occupation, seeing to it that things do not change, that they remain as they are. That is what Adam was expected to do, and part of our task in the world is indeed to guard that which we have been given: our natural environment, our social setting, our religious heritage.[13]

But there is also the task of *"'le-ovdah'* (to cultivate it), which is essentially creative: to develop, to work, to innovate."[14] How are these to be balanced?

We guard because God owns the world, and "we are never truly masters."[15] But those who guard (*shomerim*) are of various types. Some have only tasks but no rights, like a guard, while a borrower or renter has certain rights in addition to obligations.[16] If I rent a home, for example, the owner can make claims against me if I misuse the property, which is, after all, not mine; still, with respect to the property, I have claims to privacy, occupation, and use. While we do not have rights against God, says Lichtenstein, we do have "rights to use the property, given the Owner's continuing consent."[17] Consequently, in our "capacity as *shomerim*, we must live with a sense of responsibility, obligation and demands"; not merely a passivity but an "application of consciousness," an alertness in which the "human self must be asserted," guarding "with intelligence."[18]

Emphasizing the intelligent activity of the human, even as we guard/keep the garden, goes some way to solving the tension between the two mandates. One reading, says Lichtenstein, posits that in the beginning the world was created perfect, although one

13. Aharon Lichtenstein, "To Cultivate and to Guard: The Universal Duties of Mankind," adapted Reuven Ziegler, *The Israel Koschitzky Virtual Beit Midrash*, Winter 1986–87, http://vbm-torah.org/archive/develop/01develop.htm (accessed May 28, 2014).
14. Ibid.
15. Ibid.
16. Ibid.
17. Ibid.
18. Ibid; cf. Jonathan Sacks, *To Heal a Fractured World: The Ethics of Responsibility* (New York: Schocken Books, 2005).

part of that perfection was human activity itself. Even in the well-ordered garden, Adam was to cultivate the garden as part of its order; if he does not do his part "one of the pieces of the picture has fallen out, and the world is no longer perfect."[19] On this interpretation, both mandates of cultivate/till and guard/keep are tasks of maintenance, keeping the world as it was by "guarding against damage and actively working in order to replenish."[20] On another reading, "'*le-ovdah*' is a mandate to go beyond the original state of creation. '*Le-ovdah*' is not meant simply to maintain the original standard; rather, we have been given the right and the duty to try to transcend it . . . to create something better, as it were."[21]

What then of this little word "keep"? Are we to keep the garden the way a curator or librarian keeps a rare text, guarding it to ensure that no one alters it? That doesn't seem to fit with the other mandates. Instead, "keeping" seems to mean something like "developing the capacities of the earth without degrading those capacities or working at cross purposes to them." Take as an example the indication of Genesis 2:5 that while there was vegetation, given God's creative work of the third day, there was as yet no "bush of the field" or "small plant of the field" because there was "no man to work the ground." Clearly, the work would change the face of the earth: clearing vegetation, planting and harvesting crops, and eventually developing new strains and varieties of those crops. This work alters, to be sure, but an alteration actualizing the earth's own potentiality.

The comprehensive trajectory of these mandates can be differentiated by three tests of good work:

(1) Respect for the integrity of things, or *Remember You are Dust*;

(2) Respect for the integrity of systemic emergence, or *Build Soil*;

(3) Proper direction, or *Fill the Temple*.

19. Ibid.
20. Ibid.
21. Ibid.

Remember You are Dust [22]

In his response to what some call the creation story's "culture of exploitation," Joseph Ratzinger suggests that the mandates do not at all support the notion that we "submit [nature] to torture and in a wracking inquisition extract the answers from it that it would otherwise not give."[23] Instead of nature serving as a blank resource for us to use however we wish, God's "directive to humankind means that it is supposed to look after the world as God's creation, and to do so in accordance with the rhythm and the logic of creation . . . the world is to be used for what it is capable of and for what it is called to, but not for what goes against it."[24] As Genesis teaches, "the garden . . . is not a wilderness, a danger, or a threat, but a home, which shelters, nourishes, and sustains," and humans are to "recognize it as God's gift and build it up in keeping with what it was created for" rather than putting creation and nature in a position of "having to defend themselves" against humans.[25] Like Rabbi Lichtenstein, then-Cardinal Ratzinger notes that creation is God's, but emphasizes *also* the status of the world, its rhythm and logic. The first test, *the integrity of things*, assumes that the things of the world possess status, that they have a weight and logic of their own, and that our work is to act in keeping with the capacity of things.

As articulated by Ratzinger, a thing's own "rhythm and . . . logic" provides guidance and limits; work which violates the proportionality and integrity of a thing, according to that thing's own act of existence, deforms it. Thomas Aquinas thought the same, again and

---

22. Test one is a restatement of the *Catechism of the Catholic Church*, sec. 339: "Each creature possesses its own particular goodness and perfection. For each one of the works of the 'six days' it is said: 'and God saw that it was good.' 'By the very nature of creation, material being is endowed with its own stability, truth and excellence, its own order and laws.' Each of the various creatures, willed in its own being, reflects in its own way a ray of God's infinite wisdom and goodness. Man must therefore respect the particular goodness of every creature, to avoid any disordered use of things which would be in contempt of the Creator and would bring disastrous consequences for human beings and their environment."

23. Ratzinger, *In the Beginning*, 35.

24. Ibid., 34.

25. Ibid., 64, 81.

again turning to "objects in their substantial concreteness."[26] Whereas Aristotle fixated on abstract *essence*, Thomas "proposed an *existential* ontology, in which the primary value was *ipsum esse*, the concrete act of existing."[27] And, unlike Plato, who turned away from concrete things to find integrity, Aquinas turns to the individual things themselves, looking for proportion and integrity realized according to the thing's concrete act.[28]

Romano Guardini makes a similar point in *Letters from Lake Como*, explaining the difference between undeveloped nature and what he terms *urbanitas*. *Urbanitas* means "'city-living,' a city atmosphere, yet one in which a nobly shaped humanity can flourish. Here nature can pass over smoothly into culture . . . I cannot find a way to express how human this nature is. . . . Here was form closer to humanity. Here was nature indwelt by humanity."[29] As understood by Guardini, there is no human interaction with nature that does not enculturate nature, and we are always refashioning the world so as to have a *place* there; for us to be somewhere, we must indwell nature with our humanity, but we can do so in a way which is tied elastically to nature, or in a way muting nature's voice.[30]

Take a sailboat, for example. In it, wind and wood and linen are harnessed according to "an ancient legacy of form" allowing human mastery, and with this mastery comes a "certain remoteness" from nature, the mediation of our tools separating us from direct immersion.[31] Yet the distance does not silence nature: "Those who control this ship are still very closely related to the wind and waves. They are breast to breast with their force. Eye and hand and whole body brace against them. We have here real culture—elevation above nature, yet decisive nearness to it."[32] As we materialize our spirit,

26. Umberto Eco, *Art and Beauty in the Middle Ages*, trans. Hugh Bredin (New Haven: Yale University Press, 1986), 74.

27. Ibid., 75.

28. Ibid., 76.

29. Romano Guardini, *Letters from Lake Como: Explorations in Technology and the Human Race*, trans. Geoffrey W. Bromiley (Grand Rapids: Eerdmans, 1994), 6–7.

30. Ibid., 11.

31. Ibid., 12.

32. Ibid.

nature is humanized, indwelled with culture. Some work "masters" nature proportionate to nature's own capacity; while other work crushes nature, bending it to human will against the integrity of the thing—deforming the worker at the same time. Certainly, such work does not *approve* of the thing, for it does not affirm how good it is that the thing exists *as* the thing it is; instead, it tries to make the thing *other*, against the form and finality of its integrity.

God creates by approval, granting separate existence to the things created; since anything created cannot be God since God is uncreated, created entities must have their own distinct substantiality. Obviously, created entities are not self-caused or autonomous in their ability to sustain their being, which is an ongoing gift; but, nonetheless, created entities are given their own existence, form, matter (if a material entity), potentialities, operations, tendencies, and actuality. Things are created after their own kind, and this is good. So while things are not independent of God, they possess their own integrity, which is a gift itself.

Work which keeps the world acts in accordance with this integrity; it does not contravene the goodness of entities. This is not to say that such respect prohibits alteration, for transformation can perfect, just as art and grace perfect nature, or exercise perfects the body, or education perfects intelligence.[33] To act in accordance with the integrity of things is to act in attunement, but it is not to maintain the static, pristine origin of the thing.

One way to think of this would be to think of good work as *attending* to the integrity of things. In an obvious sense, attending pays attention, grasps what is there, does not overlook, or ignore. But attending also at-tends—tends to—in awareness of and care for the nature of things. This is what it means to be a husband in the agricultural sense of knowing the carrying capacity of land. When cattle are put to pasture, the good husband knows the carrying capacity of the land. Lush, rich grass might be able to handle many head of cattle to a single acre without overgrazing and destruction of the grass whereas poorer land in dryer regions might require many

---

33. In this context, "perfect" means to make complete or to bring to fruition; it is *not* equivalent to "lacking nothing."

acres for a single cow. If the husband *knows* (pays attention) and *cares* (tends), he can rotate the cattle from plot to plot in a way which provides ample nutrition for the good of the cattle without harm to the grass or the soil, and, given particularly intelligent husbandry, to the benefit of the soil and grass itself, leading to a second test of good work.

Build Soil[34]

Despite claiming that we are to keep the garden as an artist keeps a canvas and not as a curator keeps a painting, all this talk of integrity and inner rhythm and logic conveys the mood of preservation, as if we keep the garden best when maintaining it in exactly the same shape as it was given. If this were true, our goal would be akin to "leave no trace," with the best human work entirely invisible, altering nothing of the natural governance of the world. This cannot be the case if culture-making is part of the command to fill, and certainly cannot be the case if the primary purpose of labor is the perfection and development of our own subjectivity. So, while we are to respect the integrity of things without in any way violating their inner logic, such respect does not imply a resistance to developing and altering the world so long as development is in keeping with that integrity, which it is because God has created a *friendly universe.*[35]

Things do not exist in monadic isolation, pre-programmed to follow their own inner directions as if nothing else existed and with only accidental relationships or systematic integration with other things. Not at all. As created by a self-communicative God, the nature of all reality is relational, although of course things enter into relations in distinct ways, proper to their mode of being. Protons and electrons do not love each other, for instance, but they relate. Similarly, stones do not seek to be known, but they are intrinsically knowable to intelligence. Things do not exist in mutual

34. The second test restates the *Catechism of the Catholic Church*, sec. 340: "God wills the interdependence of creatures. The sun and the moon, the cedar and the little flower, the eagle and the sparrow: the spectacle of their countless diversities and inequalities tells us that no creature is self-sufficient. Creatures exist only in dependence on each other, to complete each other, in the service of each other."

35. Bernard Lonergan, *Method in Theology* (New York: Seabury Press, 1972), 117.

hostility or endless self-regard, but as members in the assembly of being(s) (*ens commune*). In a friendly or hospitable universe such as our own, preserving a thing as if it were non-relational is to violate the integrity and nature of the thing: integrity cannot be considered as an isolationist or solipsistic endeavor.

We are often tempted by a reductive vision to (a) consider knowledge attained when we have identified and isolated the constitutive parts of things and systems and (b) captured that knowledge in fixed concepts, rather like a fly in amber.[36] In such a conceptualization, "any item, be it a concept or a word, is distinguished from another by its self-reference, so that every unity is thought to be an incomplex unit, a simple self-identity . . . that excludes all others from the self-identical simplicity of each unit," as opposed to the "intrinsically and really complex" understanding of being present in medieval modes of thought.[37] But this is not true. For, as complex and relational, things function in a dynamic way allowing further relations and systems to result; the logic or rhythm of creation is developmental and emergent rather than static or frozen.[38]

New systems and substances emerge from the functions of other systems, even though this emergence is governed by structures of probability rather than sheer necessity. For instance, the presence of liquid water and solar heat on a planet allows for the recurrent operations of evaporation and condensation. In time, as the atmosphere stabilizes and a statistically normal range of high and low temperatures results, a hydrological system emerges, and as the pattern of precipitation and evaporation relates to land masses with their various elevations, the hydrologic system influences erosion, run-off, sediment formation and so on, until the conditions are met

36. Consider the projects of Bacon or Descartes, for instance.
37. Schmitz, *Recovery of Wonder*, 51.
38. What follows borrows liberally from the thought of Bernard Lonergan, *Collected Works of Bernard Lonergan*, ed. Frederick E. Crowe and Robert M. Doran, vol. 3, *Insight: A Study in Human Understanding* (Toronto: University of Toronto, 1992), esp. 141–62. Also R.J. Snell, *Through a Glass Darkly: Bernard Lonergan and Richard Rorty on Knowing without a God's-Eye View* (Milwaukee: Marquette University Press, 2006).

allowing terrestrial life to emerge.[39] At the same time, terrestrial life does not follow simply from hydrological systems but requires similarly complex recurrent schemes in several physical and chemical systems. Incredibly complex and interrelated while allowing the function of things and systems in their own right, the entire process is one of emergent probability where "simpler" systems help create the conditions for greater complexity, even as the more complex systems are not reducible to the laws and principles of the lower. Human consciousness, for example, is possible only because of non-conscious chemical and physical properties, but consciousness in no way can be reduced to chemistry. Consequently, multiple recurrent schemes, each operating in their own way according to their own dynamic possibilities, interrelate in a variety of ways to allow for the emergence of new systems and substances not present in the original schemes.

While not articulated in the same language, the basic heuristic of a dynamic and developmental world process was already known to St. Augustine, and is perfectly at home in the Christian understanding of creation, as Rowan Williams explains:

> Creation is ... the setting in being of a living system designed to grow toward beauty and order, even if this beauty and order is not at any given moment fully apparent ... it is a world in motion, a set of processes in which potential is realized. This idea is developed ... through the concept of *rationes causales* or *rationes seminales*, terms that ... represent the latent power of development in created things. However, this should not be understood to mean that things are created simply with immanent capacities for growth, and that their subsequent history does not more than unfold what has been there from the beginning in terms of natural processes. The *rationes* do indeed contain the potential in things for natural development, but they also specify the ways in which things in the world may be acted upon by God.[40]

39. Kenneth R. Melchin, *History, Ethics, and Emergent Probability: Ethics, Society and History in the Work of Bernard Lonergan*, 2nd edition (The Lonergan Website, 1999), 109.

40. Rowan Williams, "Creation," in *Augustine through the Ages: An Encyclopedia*, gen. ed. Allan D. Fitzgerald (Grand Rapids: Eerdmans, 1999), 252.

Note that Augustine understands the developmental power of creation as present rather than alien to the capacities of created things; they possess, in their own integrity, the capacities for growth, not toward their own actualization alone, but also in contributing to the perfection of the whole. A thing may go beyond its own immanent act without thereby violating the integrity of that act, even if the emergence is somewhat open-ended, not following of sheer logical necessity in only one direction. Part of the integrity of things includes contributing to the ongoing dynamism of the universe.

Further, as Augustine understands it, this same developmental integrity is, by its own nature, open to God's act, yet in no way can God's act be reduced to the thing's own potency. Still, God's "external" act does not violate the thing, even while going beyond it, for grace, similar to art, perfects rather than harms nature. Now, since God often acts through the secondary causation of human agency—filling the world, in part, through human work—our labor can be God's way of developing the *rationes*. In other words, in the friendly universe, the human ability and need to augment creation can be perfectly in keeping with the integrity of things. In fact, the absence of human development could itself be a lacuna for the well-being of things, as evidenced by the creation account of Genesis in which God's art allowed for the emergence of responsible moral agents from brute matter—*adam* from *adamah*—so the garden could be governed, worked, kept, and filled properly.

Moreover, since Adam emerges from chemical and physical systems, without in any way reducing to those systems *and* without minimizing God's creative role in human emergence—Adam is born of dirt and God's breath—human development of nature is the means by which nature develops itself. While humanity is not brute matter without a spiritual principle, we are not separated from or alien to nature. We come from the dirt and for the dirt, after all, resulting from God's choice to elevate the dirt to personal responsibility, and so our subsequent digging and shaping of dirt into pottery or bricks is an aspect in the emergent probability immanent to nature itself. Consequently, we cannot respect the integrity of things without developing them, for they have an inner tendency toward development, and any squelching of our own drive to better the garden would violate the garden inasmuch as it represses our own, natural integrity.[41]

Explaining this much more concretely, Michael Pollan tells of the grass on a well-managed farm. While some might consider an ungrazed pasture to be optimal, this is not the case, for under-grazing is almost as damaging to the grass and soil as overgrazing. Intelligent use *improves* the soil beyond what it would be if merely left fallow. When the cow grazes, it "appears to have diminished the pasture," but in reality grazing

> sets into motion a sequence of events that will confer a measurable benefit on this square foot of pasture. The shorn grass plant, endeavoring to restore the rough balance between its roots and leaves, will proceed to shed as much root mass as it's just lost in leaf mass. When the discarded roots die, the soil's resident population of bacteria, fungi, and earthworms will get to work breaking them down into rich grown humus.... It is in this manner that the grazing of ruminants, when managed properly, actually builds new soil from the bottom up. Organic matter in a pasture also builds from the top down, as leaf litter and animal wastes break down on the surface, much as it does on a forest floor. But in a grassland decaying roots are the biggest source of new organic matter, and in the absence of grazers the soil-building process would be nowhere near as swift of productive.[42]

By attending, human work betters the entire system, allowing each aspect of it to flourish as the system itself develops and emerges. As articulated by Wendell Berry, this comprehensive interaction is the Great Economy, the Kingdom of God, including *everything* in relation to *everything*:

> the first principle of the Kingdom of God is that it includes everything; in it, the fall of every sparrow is a significant event.... Another principle ... is that everything in the Kingdom of God is

---

41. That Adam obeys God in his energetic and dynamic capacity of subduing the world with technology and industry is articulated profoundly by Rabbi Joseph Soloveitchik, see *The Lonely Man of Faith* (New York: Three Leaves Press, 1965).

42. Michael Pollan, *The Omnivore's Dilemma: A Natural History of Four Meals* (New York: Penguin Books, 2006), 196.

joined both to it and to everything else that is in it; that is to say, the Kingdom of God is orderly. A third principle is that humans do not and can never know either all the creatures that the Kingdom of God contains or the whole pattern of order by which it contains them.[43]

This order, or *pattern*, is "greater and more intricate than we can know," and so our actions are matters of "an extremity of seriousness and an extremity of humility."[44]

Berry also uses topsoil as an example; for, like the Great Economy itself, we cannot make it, although we can build it "by assenting to, preserving, and perhaps collaborating in its own processes."[45] Unlike the usual understanding, soil is not just dirt, for "a handful of the real thing has life in it; it is full of living creatures" and "behaves complexly and wonderfully."[46] Healthy topsoil drains well and holds water, and thus provides water supply for crops while controlling floods. Made of various life forms dying and living, it is "a graveyard, a place of resurrection, and a community of living creatures"—and everything else depends upon it.[47] More, when human labor operates in keeping with the capacity and order of soil and the limits and capacity of other things as they relate to the soil—animals, irrigation, logging, manure, tilling—this work builds up the whole system of soil; but insofar as human actions work against these ordering principles, the soil is weakened, dies, erodes, blows, as also the many other dependent elements. Topsoil takes decades and centuries to build even an inch, but can be lost through bad management in an afternoon. But if the soil is maintained, agriculture emerges; if agriculture is maintained, *urbanitas* emerges, along with all the benefits and goods of advanced (emergent) culture. Insofar as we keep the soil alive, we can enjoy economy, advanced governance, the arts, and so forth; but should the soil die, we revert to unsuccessful hunter-gatherers. From soil, humans emerge; from humans, agriculture

---

43. Wendell Berry, *The Art of the Commonplace: The Agrarian Essays of Wendell Berry*, ed. Norman Wirzba (Washington, DC: Shoemaker & Hoard, 2002), 219–20.
44. Ibid., 220–21.
45. Ibid., 225.
46. Ibid., 225–26.
47. Ibid., 228.

emerges, potentially bettering the soil; with better soil, the leisure for advanced culture, including arts, literature, theology, and the university; with advanced culture, the education of humans and the development of agriculture; with the education of humans and new agriculture, the soil is bettered. In a friendly and rational universe, this pattern continues in a positive feedback loop.

Of course, the joker in the deck is that we are not always rational, often deliberately and sinfully so. Bad management of soil—or anything else—brings costs, and not merely to the thing but to the whole pattern. Poor managers, whether so by ignorance or greed, tend to assume that invisible costs "downstream" are not costs at all since they have no obvious consequence, while the principles of the Great Economy, on the other hand, posit that there are costs to everything.[48] The account is never closed merely because the cost is not obvious. Everything effects everything in ways great or small, and the comprehensiveness of the Great Economy reckons the balance, even if unknown to us.[49] Husbands work within pattern, in concern for *health* of the whole, knowing much of it lies outside their knowledge but within their concern and responsibility.[50]

Fill the Temple [51]

Since sin impairs the function of the friendly universe, a third test is necessary, although without sin the first two tests would be suffi-

48. A similar point about the blindness of a certain kind of management is made by Alasdair MacIntyre, *After Virtue: A Study in Moral Theory* (Notre Dame: University of Notre Dame Press, 1984).

49. Berry, *Art of the Commonplace*, 233.

50. Ibid., 267–75.

51. Test three restates the *Catechism of the Catholic Church*, sec. 358: "God created everything for man, but man in turn was created to serve and love God and to offer all creation back to him: What is it that is about to be created, that enjoys such honor? It is man that great and wonderful living creature, more precious in the eyes of God than all other creatures! For him the heavens and the earth, the sea and all the rest of creation exist. God attached so much importance to his salvation that he did not spare his own Son for the sake of man. Nor does he ever cease to work, trying every possible means, until he has raised man up to himself and made him sit at his right hand."

cient with normal human functioning. Because we are abnormal, under the reign of sin, work requires an eschatological test as well. Tasked with the mandate to fill, we need ask whether our work would appropriately fill God's palace (Is 60:6–7), or be better consigned to the markets of Babylon.

If God as a wise king fills his temple, including the New Jerusalem, with good things, and if God has willed to accomplish this filling partly through the sub-creation of human labor, then there is little reason to think that the products of human work will be destroyed or rendered irrelevant in the end. Rather, if the fruits of good labor—both the objective products and the subjective development of the human person—could be presented to God as adornments for his temple, then the implications of work become quite significant. Is this the sort of work I could present to God and God's people as a "house warming" gift which would adorn the halls of the temple forever? That's something of a weighty question, hence "the expectation of the eschatological transformation invests human work with ultimate significance. Through it human beings contribute in their modest and broken way to God's new creation."[52]

This is not to say that humans do not need grace for good work or that the products of our labor would not need some sort of gracious redemption or transformation. It is to say that God can redeem and transform our work, that even swords and spears can be transformed into plowshares and pruning hooks for use in the garden-city (Is 2:4):

> Not all of the items of pagan culture will be gathered *as is* into the Holy City. A pagan ship will be changed into a redeemed ship— but it will still be a ship. But other things will have to have their identities, their basic functions, transformed; some of them will be changed almost beyond recognition . . . the emphasis here is on transformation, not destruction.[53]

Now, even if God can redeem work, the test would remain: does this work have its natural home in Babylon? If so, it is bad work. Given

52. Volf, *Work in the Spirit*, 92.
53. Mouw, *When the Kings Come Marching In*, 40–41.

sin, much of our work is bad, but our work is not necessarily bad, and certainly not irredeemable.

Rabbi Jonathan Sacks provides a brilliant example of this in explaining the relationship between divine and human initiative at Sinai and the construction of the Tabernacle. God has revealed himself at Sinai—for Jews the "greatest epiphany in history"[54]—yet when Moses stays too long on the mountain, the people convince Aaron to make the golden calf. God has revealed himself in an abiding covenant, but at the first worry they revert to paganism: "Up, make us gods, who shall go before us; as for this Moses, the man who brought us up out of the land of Egypt, we do not know what has become of him" (Ex 32:1). Moses, told by God of this apostasy, rushes down the mountain in a fury. First, he destroys the tablets on which God himself had written the commandments—"the writing was the writing of God, graven upon the tables" (Ex 32:16)—then smashes the golden calf, grinds it to powder, casts the powder into water and makes the Israelites drink.

Returning to the mountain to beg forgiveness for the people, Moses receives the instruction to make a second set of commandments, this time hewn by his own hand. On the face of it, this is a remarkable loss, the originals are gone, replaced with a copy partially constructed by Moses; the content is identical, but the direct hand of God is lessened. Yet, when Moses descends the mountain this time, his face is radiant: "What is intriguing, however, is the fact that Moses did *not* radiate when he brought down the first tablets, but on the second occasion he did."[55] The first tablets do not survive, but the second set, "the result of a partnership between Moses and God" does survive, and "Moses himself was changed as the result of the participation."[56] While he had been largely passive in receiving the first set, here, by God's own invitation and command, he was active and Moses was changed. Oddly, and in a particular way, the second set was better, or at least better for humanity, precisely because Moses labored, because of human work.

---

54. Sacks, *To Heal a Fractured World*, 148.
55. Ibid., 148–49.
56. Ibid.

Sacks notes a similar transition between passivity and activity in the people as well.[57] In preparation for Sinai, the people did nothing other than to purify themselves and wait for God to reveal himself, even kept away from the mountain; but after the golden calf, the work of constructing the tabernacle occupies them and they are busy making a place for God. Even the instructions for the tabernacle reveal the change. At Sinai, the people remain at the foot of the mountain, corresponding to the tabernacle's outer court; the priests and elders proceed up the mountain slope while Moses alone goes to the summit, just as the Holy Place welcomes the priests and the Holy of Holies is reserved for the High Priest alone.[58] A cloud covers the mountain and tent; God is present in the cloud and Moses cannot draw near until God speaks, then the glory of God appears as fire visible to all the people and Moses (with Aaron at the tabernacle) enters into the presence.[59] According to Sacks, the "implication is radical and unmistakable: *Creating the universe, God made a home for human beings. Making the sanctuary, human beings made a home for God.*"[60]

As a Christian, I recognize the same pattern of humans making a place for God to reside, not only in the tabernacle and temple, but most fully in the womb of Mary who cooperates with the Holy Spirit—"Let it be done to me according to your word. And the Word was made flesh"—and in bread and wine, work of human hands, which becomes that same Word. Without human agency, God does not take up residence among us, either in Bethlehem or at the altar: "God does not come to us through a creation of nature alone, holy trees, water or fire. God comes to us through the first creation of culture—bread and wine."[61] God fills his temple with his presence, and he fills his Cosmic Temple with the works of our hands, choosing even to adorn his eternal city with us and our works.

---

57. Ibid., 151–52.
58. Ibid., 151.
59. Ibid., 152.
60. Ibid., 151.
61. Tischner, *Spirit of Solidarity*, 97.

Conclusion

We have, then, three tests of good work: (1) Does it respect the integrity of things, including the integrity of the worker? (2) Does it contribute to the capacity of the created order, including the human person, for dynamic development and intelligent progress? (3) Does the work suit the feasting halls of New Jerusalem or the gluttonous meals of Babylon? Remarkably, keeping these tests allows us to cooperate in our own subjective perfection—becoming fully alive—as developing and improving the world itself, to the delight of God who fills his palace with our work. Working for the dirt from which we are formed makes us fit governors, even while elevating the dirt into vessels fit for God's own presence.

Part Two

The Unbearable Weightiness of Being

3

Hating Being:
Sloth, Boredom, Nihilism

Humans face the world with a particular stance and from a particular position. Unlike an observant but static camera, we dwell in the world in a variety of moods and positions, changing not just ourselves but our worlds as we do so. If our stance toward the world is one of eager and passionate interest, the world sparkles and captivates; if we aggressively seek profit and gain, the world appears as resource; if we are bored, the world fails to engage.

This is true for every person, and since each takes a particular stance at a given time, we will not inhabit identical worlds—yours is now captivating, mine is now an irritant—even while near each other in space and time, perhaps even in the presence of each other. Still, despite the particular experience of each person, social and historical tendencies emerge whereby persons in one cultural space share a similar stance.

Charles Taylor illustrates this by noting the difference between an enchanted and disenchanted world.[1] The pre-modern person lived in an enchanted world where meaning was thought to reside in things themselves—the world was full, sometimes frighteningly full, of meaning. A bone fragment from a saint retained the sanctity and curative power of the saint, rogation days were good days for planting, and a procession of the Virgin's image could drive evil spirits away, for things possessed their own meanings and powers and humans lived alongside those meanings rather than creating

---

1. Charles Taylor, *A Secular Age*, 25–38.

them.[2] An enchanted culture experienced the world as "charged," full of meaning, and thus to be respected. Things are quite different for the contemporary Western person occupying a disenchanted world where things mean only what we assign them (or so it is thought).

So while a medieval could feel irritated or angry or greedy, just like a modern, the conditions of belief have changed so substantially between that charged religious world and this disenchanted secular world as to change the meanings of those stances. If one was irritated at the order of the cosmos in 1066, one was irritated, in a very real sense, at the ordering chosen by God; postmodern irritation is directed at nothing, just a coldly impersonal set of forces. The historical and social situation has changed the meaning of our possible stances toward the world, and, correspondingly, to the various meanings of our worlds.

In these next two chapters I suggest that the stance toward the world most evident in the historical and social space of contemporary Western life is a stance of bored sloth. Moderns struggle to find the world beautiful, or good, or of worth, and once the world and the things of the world are thought worthless in themselves, they bore us. Further, we struggle to find worth in other persons or ourselves. However horrifying, we find this boredom impossible to give up—we like the boredom—because the meaninglessness of the world allows us to treat it and others and ourselves exactly as we wish. Like Judge Holden, we are terribly free; since the world, for us, does not have the weight of glory, we owe it nothing and can do with it precisely as we wish, or as John Paul II stated, we "end by detaching human freedom from its essential and constitutive relationship to truth."[3] Further, as he noted so often, a culture of freedom without truth, a culture where freedom is unchecked by the

---

2. Consider the popular beliefs associated with Candlemas in the late medieval period whereby the candles themselves were thought capable of protecting people from storm, sickness, and devil, or, if used by witches, of bringing harm and torment. See Eamon Duffy, *The Stripping of the Altars: Traditional Religion in England c. 1400–1580* (New Haven: Yale University Press, 1992), 16–19.

3. John Paul II, *Veritatis Splendor*, 4.

good of being, becomes a culture of death. Our bored culture is a culture actively engaging in a revolt against limits, place, order, and thus willing to harm and kill our world, each other—especially the weakest among us—in a pique of freedom.

To live in a disenchanted, unencumbered world of freedom intoxicates us, to be sure, but it also casts us adrift existentially, morally, and spiritually. "What are we to do?" "What are we for?" "What is the good life?"—these and other questions are direction-less in a culture where freedom itself is a final authority, especially freedom lacking definition. We simply do not know why we exist, and we hate any answer that might compel us to limit our empty freedom and actually attain the good. Freedom is for us, now, an idol, and our conception of freedom is so absolute that we increas-ingly perceive limits as illicit and impermissible—"it is forbidden to forbid." So total are the demands of our new god that even our own human nature is thought a trap. Our new freedom, this freedom from dwelling in the density of being, is a prison. Flattened and unhooked from reality, lives are arbitrary and insignificant, and only an increasingly shrill insistence of significance remains—an insistence bearing no weight. This weightlessness, this unbearable lightness of being, results in the torpor of meaninglessness, the spir-itually enervating results of a life not worth living.

Christian tradition provides a fascinating account of a particular vice, *acedia*, usually translated as sloth, which seems to capture with particular aptness the spiritual conditions of our own age.[4] No longer a vice afflicting individuals only, *acedia* has become a cul-tural reality; nestled deep in the roots of our ways of acting and liv-ing, sloth seeps into our loves and lives in virtually every domain, before finally transforming itself into boredom and nihilism.

---

4. For a similar claim, see Paul J. Wadell and Darin H. Davis, "Tracking the Tox-ins of *Acedia*: Reenvisioning Moral Education," in *The Schooled Heart: Moral For-mation in American Higher Education*, eds. Michael D. Beaty and Douglas V. Henry (Waco: Baylor University Press, 2007), 133–34.

Disgust at Being

Acedia receives extensive discussion in early monastic literature.[5] Evagrius of Ponticus considered it the most troublesome of the "demonic thoughts," a judgment shared with John Cassian, John Climacus, and others:[6]

> He attacks the monk about the fourth hour and besieges his soul until the eighth hour. First he makes the sun appear sluggish and immobile, as if the day had fifty hours. Then he causes the monk continuously to look at the windows and forces him to step out of his cell and to gaze at the sun to see how far it still is from the ninth hour, and to look around, here and there, whether any of his brethren is near. Moreover, the demon sends him hatred against the place, against life itself, and against the work of his hands, and makes him think he has lost the love among his brethren and that there is none to comfort him. . . . He stirs the monk also to long for different places in which he can find easily what is necessary for his life and can carry on a much less toilsome and more expedient profession.[7]

A wide range of effects follows: sleepiness, sickness, inattentiveness, dissatisfaction, a feeling of tedium, restlessness, wanderlust, hatred

---

5. Andrew Crislip, "The Sin of Sloth or the Illness of the Demons? The Demon of Acedia in Early Christian Monasticism," *Harvard Theological Review* 98:2 (2005): 146–153; Placide Deseille, "Acedia According to the Monastic Tradition," *Cisterian Studies Quarterly* 37:3 (2002): 297–301; Jean-Charles Nault, "Acedia: Enemy of Spiritual Joy," *Communio* 31 (Summer 2004): 236–58; Reinhard Kuhn, *The Demon of Noontide: Ennui in Western Literature* (Princeton: Princeton University Press, 1976); Patricia Meyer Spacks, *Boredom: The Literary History of a State of Mind* (Chicago: University of Chicago Press, 1995); Elizabeth S. Goodstein, *Experience Without Qualities: Boredom and Modernity* (Stanford: Stanford University Press, 2005); Michael Hanby, "The Culture of Death, the Ontology of Boredom, and the Resistance of Joy," *Communio* 31 (2004): 181–99.

6. Crislip, "Sin of Sloth," 143, note 1; John Cassian, *The Institutes*, trans. Boniface Ramsey, O.P., vol. 58 of *Ancient Christian Writers*, ed. Dennis D. McManus (New York: Newman Press, 2000), 217–36; John Cassian, *The Conferences*, trans. Boniface Ramsey, O.P., vol. 57 of *Ancient Christian Writers*, ed. Walter Burghardt, John Dillon, and Dennis D. McManus (New York: Paulist Press, 1997), 183–206.

7. In Siegfried Wenzel, *The Sin of Sloth*, 5.

for place, prideful and frenetic activity, floating from task to task.[8] Sloth is not just laziness, and while the term does come to mean mere inactivity in time, *acedia* has nothing to do with "a concept of the middle-class work ethic."[9] Rather it reveals a movement of frustration and hate—the monk actively hates, as Evagrius put it, his place and "even life itself."[10] He will feel an overwhelming desire to cease the work at hand, to leave his cell in search of conversation, or new work, or a new cell. A feeling of alienation from the work, place, and community often follows, accompanied by a feeling of disgust and revulsion, culminating in a desire to escape from the cloister and the monastic life entirely.[11]

Acedia reveals a certain internal instability—a hatred of the place, the work, and even life itself—manifested in the external instability of movement and departure. The internal instability is fundamentally a destructive hatred of whatever particular good is given to the monk by God; in *acedia* the monk longs for a better place because he "abhors what is there and fantasizes about what is not."[12] In sloth, we abhor what is there; we abhor what is; we abhor limits, place, order, being. Our misguided addiction to freedom without truth is a revolt of the self against any charged world which might demand attendance, care, obligation, or respect, and certainly any mandate of working to fill God's beautiful kingdom. These are seen as insufferable demands, as illegitimate restrictions of our unbridled freedom, and so we find ourselves hating the place God has provided, the work God has given to us, and the proper ways of laboring. Given this disgust and hatred of the truth of being, we are stricken with *acedia*, which becomes a form of infidelity, a breaking of troth, a loathing of truth. The best remedy against sloth, at least according to Evagrius, is a remedy our freedom would find disgust-

8. Pieper lists six primary markers in *Faith, Hope, and Love*, 120–21: despair, restlessness, torpor toward salvation, pusillanimity, rancor, and malice.
9. Pieper, *Faith, Hope, Love*, 118; cf. St. Gregory the Great, *Pastoral Care*, trans. Henry Davis, S.J., Vol. 11 of *Ancient Christian Writers*, ed. Johannes Quasten and Joseph C. Plumpe (New York: Newman Press, 1950), 134–36.
10. Nault, "Acedia," 240.
11. Crislip, "Sin of Sloth," 150–51.
12. Nault, "Acedia," 240.

ing, for keeping yoked, remaining faithful, is unbearable to us who
are unbearably light.[13]

Sadness at the Good

Thomas Aquinas retains something of Evagrius's understanding of
the hatred of place by identifying in sloth (1) a sadness at the divine
good (*tristitia de bono divino*) and (2) an aversion to acting (*taedium operandi*).[14]

The divine good at which sloth feels sorrow is communion with
God, at being linked in loving, intimate union with God. Since
union with God is our happiness and joy, sloth not only rejects joy
but finds the possibility of joy a deep sorrow. Humans are by nature
oriented towards the pursuit of their happiness—our loves are created to seek joy as a natural desire—and consequently sloth is a
rejection of our own loves. If our loves are created to take joy in the
good of Divine Communion, and the slothful feel only sadness
when presented with such joy, then sloth is sadness about our own
loves, a revulsion and sorrow about our own happiness—"sadness
at the Divine Good about which charity rejoices (*tristari de bono
divino, de quo caritas guadet*)."[15]

Fleeing from an internal and spiritual good is remarkably absurd
—why would anyone reject and feel disgust at the possibility of her
own fulfillment?[16] Why would anyone choose the profound self-
contradiction of loathing his own good?[17] Aquinas gives a hint at
the answer when he suggests the cure for *acedia*: "to repel this [*acedia*], the wise man advises in Ecclesiasticus (6, 26), 'Bow down thy
shoulder, and bear her (wisdom), and be not grieved (*accedieris*)
with her bands.'"[18] If *acedia* is repelled by accepting the bands or

13. Ibid., 239.
14. Aquinas, *ST* II–II. 35. 1–4. For discussion, see Wenzel, *The Sin of Sloth* 47–60
and Nault, "Acedia," 241–48.
15. Ibid., II–II. 35. 1. See also Rebecca Konyndyk DeYoung, "Resistance to the
Demands of Love: Aquinas on the Vice of *Acedia*," *The Thomist* 68 (2004): 173–204.
16. Thomas Aquinas, *On Evil*, trans. Jean Oesterle (Notre Dame: University of
Notre Dame Press, 1995), 11. 2.
17. Ibid., 11. 3.
18. Ibid.

bonds of wisdom, then it is welcomed by refusing to give up one's lightness—inordinate love of freedom and *acedia* seem to go together. Sloth resists friendship with God because of the "burdens of commitment" that such a friendship and its concomitant trans- formations of self would require.[19] In love with freedom, the sloth- ful are saddened at the costs of friendship with God—the ultimate Good—and so judge the good to be contrary to their (weightlessly free) selves:

> There is not only an investment of time, but an investment of self that is required for the relationship to exist and, further, to flour- ish. Even more difficult . . . are the accommodations of identity: from the perspective of individual "freedom," to be in this rela- tionship will change me and cost me.[20]

This self-contradiction—sadness about the good—has the fur- ther result of crippling action, of "immobiliz[ing] the person."[21] The slothful have an aversion to acting (*taedium operandi*)—that is, an aversion to good work, our *telos*. The acceptance of our task to labor is an act of will to bear the yoke, to persevere in the labor that God has given. But performing good work requires a transforma- tion of self, possible only with an acceptance of God's grace and friendship.[22] To reject God's friendship and the gift of God's own self which renders such friendship possible also rejects our capacity to cooperate with the transformative work of the Spirit which makes our good work possible: "If Christian mundane work is work in the Spirit, then it must be understood as cooperation with God. Cha- risma is not just a call by which God bids us to perform a particular task, but it is also an inspiration and a gifting to accomplish the task."[23] Sadness about the order of love cripples action, moreover, since the ultimate purpose of an act is not self-contained but judged insofar as it cooperates or resists the Spirit's work of attracting us to

19. DeYoung, "Aquinas on *Acedia*," 192, 196–97.
20. Ibid., 198.
21. Aquinas, *On Evil*, 11. 4.
22. Nault, "Acedia," 244–45.
23. Volf, *Work in the Spirit*, 98–102, 113–22, at 114.

God.[24] Rejecting the divine good evacuates purpose and ability as it jettisons the end of the act, friendship with God, leaving only our self-love, a self-love at odds with the divine good which is our final good and joy:

> Acedia . . . is a profound withdrawal into self. Action is no longer perceived as a gift of oneself, as the response to a prior love that calls us, enables our action, and makes it possible. It is seen instead as an uninhibited seeking of personal satisfaction in the fear of "losing" something. The desire to save one's "freedom" at any price reveals, in reality, a deeper enslavement to the "self." There is no longer any room for an abandonment of the self to the other or for the joy of gift; what remains is sadness or bitterness within the one who distances himself from the community and who, being separated from others, finds himself likewise separated from God.[25]

This is not to say that the slothful are not busy doing things, even working; Evagrius claims, in fact, that the slothful are often in a frenzy of action—now this, now that—in their disgust and abhorrence at what God mandates. We might actually anticipate the slothful individual and culture to be very busy, and, as the purposelessness and arbitrary nature of their business is revealed, to be ever more distracted, exhausted, and bitter in the unending attempt to express and display freedom without humility before the yokes of place, limits, order. There will not be good work, there will not be the leisure of exultation in the delight of work, but there might be a culture of total work, of the complete victory of grasping, making, producing, developing, buying and selling—and all for nought.[26]

Boredom: The Weightless Prison

Boredom has a history. The term itself did not exist until the eighteenth century and was not used regularly until the nineteenth—the Oxford English Dictionary records a letter by the Earl of Carlisle

---

24. Nault, "Acedia," 244–45.
25. Ibid., 245–46.
26. Josef Pieper, *Leisure the Basis of Culture*, trans. Alexander Dru (New York: Mentor-Omega Books, 1963), 19–23.

in 1768 about his friends who are bored by Frenchmen. This boredom was new, "different from the dullness, lassitude and tedium people had no doubt been experiencing for centuries."[27] Boredom, then, is a phenomenon of modernity, in some sense possible only in the disenchanted world of modernity.[28] Of course one imagines that medieval students found time moving slowly in much the same way as our own students do, and certainly "situative boredom" is a constant of the human experience.[29] In situative boredom, one is bored because of something "specific in a situation"[30]—the homilist drones on, one's date boasts of their video game prowess, and so on. In the face of tedium, we wish for time to be whiled away, as when people waiting for a flight watch the clock, check the departure time, browse the magazine rack, play on their phone ... then the clock again, all in great consternation that only three minutes have elapsed—they want time to disappear. Martin Heidegger describes this as "being bored with something."[31]

A second form, what Heidegger terms "boring oneself with something" is also universal.[32] Boring oneself with something is an odd phrase, but we understand it. Recall the experience of enjoying yourself at a party that was by all accounts a success—the food was good, the music enjoyable, the companionship fine, and a friend arrived unexpectedly. Still, in the post-party reverie you conclude that you were bored the entire time, although you're not sure why.[33] In situative boredom you knew what bored you—the wait for the plane, the topic of conversation, the sales pitch. The party, however, did not prompt you to look at your watch or daydream of escape, but later you realize its emptiness. Time was filled well, you did not wish it to be whiled away, but the party did not satisfy, it did not ful-

---

27. Jennifer Schuessler, "Our Boredom, Ourselves," *New York Times*, January 21, 2010, http://www.nytimes.com/2010/01/24/books/review/Schuessler-t.html.

28. Lars Svendsen, *A Philosophy of Boredom* (London: Reaktion Books, 2005), 11, 20–26.

29. Ibid., 21.

30. Ibid.

31. Ibid., 119.

32. Ibid.

33. Ibid., 119–20.

fill. On the way home, perhaps, you resolve to do more with your life than attend dinner parties.[34] It was fun, you enjoyed it, but there's a strange remorse and listlessness afterwards, even a kind of repugnance at having gone, and especially for having thought it so enjoyable: "Why did I like that? What was the point of it?"

The third form of boredom identified by Heidegger is being bored by boredom itself. In other boredoms one is bored by the emptiness of objects, situations, and activities, but in this third boredom everything leaves one empty, including, and perhaps especially, one's own self. Bored with everything, there is no hiding place, no ability to lose oneself in any interesting and distracting reality, and one is, says Heidegger, compelled to listen. To what? Listen to what? To the indifference of it all. To the meaninglessness of everything, even the meaninglessness of our own existence. When distracted by this or that, it is easy enough to slumber through reality with incredible lightness because everything distracts just enough to allow us to not recognize its pointlessness. Profound boredom forces an encounter with the task of becoming one's own self, an inversion of Adam's response ("At last!") to appropriating his own subjectivity.

Essential boredom sees everything (not just this tedious thing) as meaningless, resulting in normlessness or anomie, with an increasing need for distraction, for ways to fill the time, or perhaps "to kill time."

> The pell-mell rush for diversions precisely indicates our fear of the emptiness that surrounds us. This rush, the demand for satisfaction and the lack of satisfaction are inextricably intertwined. The more strongly individual life becomes the centre of focus, the stronger the insistence on meaning amongst the trivialities of everyday life will become ... everyday life now appears to be a prison. Boredom is not connected with actual needs but with desire.[35]

Everyday life is a prison, but a weightless prison, revealing the lightness of our everyday existence—the lack of significance of ourselves,

---

34. Ibid.
35. Ibid., 27.

our events, and the things of the world. It reveals that things are without value, and although they can serve as objects of desire and interest us enough to distract us or incite our wants, they are, in themselves, without value:

> an object without quality is an object without identity. For earlier societies, things were bearers of continuity and stability, but this is the diametric opposite of the principle of fashion ... to make an object superfluous as soon as possible, so as to be able to move on to a new one.[36]

In *Lost in the Cosmos*, Walker Percy suggests that "there is no fashion so absurd, even grotesque, that it cannot be adopted, given two things: the authority of the fashion-trendsetter ... and the vacuity or noughtness of the consumer."[37] In order for the tyranny of fashion to reign, there must be a sense that the self is lacking something, and that wholeness might be possible with the object of fashion, especially those fashions presented by the authority of the trend-setter, for they seem to have something lacking—a self. Percy suggests six stages of consumption and desire as relevant to fashion. First, you see a trendsetter wearing the item, but it seems outlandish and even ugly—it is most definitely not "you." Second, ordinary people are wearing the fashion—it is still not you, but the item is something and without it you are beginning to recede into noughtness. Third, you try it on. The clerk says, "it's so you," and you begin to perceive that it could be you. Fourth, it is purchased. It is you, and with great conspicuousness you wear it for the first time, aware that everyone finally sees you. Fifth, it becomes usual, everyday. You are beginning to devour its being. Sixth, it is consumed and out of fashion. You have absorbed its being and it is now evacuated as an object, but so are you evacuated. Like a vampire, you lived by consumption, but the source of life is now consumed. Need proof? Look at an old picture of yourself and note the confused embarrassment—"Who is that person? It's not really me."

36. Ibid., 46.
37. Walker Percy, *Lost in the Cosmos: The Last Self-Help Book* (New York: Picador, 1983), 23.

When one is unbearably light, the self is a prison, the self is nothing, and new and interesting desires are necessary to provide a simulacra of self, but in the third stage of boredom, even these self-sustaining desires are recognized as pointless:

> We are desperate in our search for differences. Fortunately, or regrettably, the advertising industry is there to save us with new distinctions. Advertising is essentially nothing more than creating qualitative differences where there are none. Most products ... are almost completely identical for that reason, it becomes even more important to create a difference that can distinguish products from one another ... for by establishing such differences we hope to maintain a belief that the world still has qualities.[38]

Knowing full well that things lack qualities, the meaning of desire is lost, the self is nothing, but still the self is a potentiality. We are free, but what's the point?

Nihilism: The Noughting of it All

As Evagrius and Aquinas show, sloth enervates the meaning of desire and the point of action. For the slothful, embedding the self in the mandates of good work occasions sorrow and repugnance, even horror. The slothful self considers freedom possible only on the condition that will is limited by nothing other than the will itself—and here we discover nihilism lurking with boredom as sloth's companions:

> Nihilism is a hatred of being, a dis-location of the human person from the universe of being, that is, an uprooting of man from his proper place: in a word, it is man's departure from his home.... Indeed, nihilism views reality as unintelligible, deprived of meaning in and for itself: the very concept of truth is refused as nonsense, meaningless.... *Acedia* exhibits the desire to get rid of God. Man has attempted to assert his self-creation, yet the result has only been non-sense.[39]

In the face of this non-sense, desire is reduced and nihilistic:

38. Svendsen, *Boredom*, 47.
39. Nault, "Acedia," 249.

[such] culture . . . assumes that our lives are innately and intrinsically meaningless without the constant stream of "stimulation" and distraction, a stream inevitably subject to the law of diminishing returns. This nullity on the side of the subject is matched by a similar noughting in the world, for latent in this assumption is a corollary denial of form, objective beauty, or a true order of goods that naturally and of themselves compels our interest. As a consequence, according to this cultural logic, all such choices can only be indifferently related to one another. None is intrinsically good or bad, and indeed no good approaches that of choice itself. Hence most citizens of the modern West, almost of necessity, live lives of profound fragmentation and internal contradiction.[40]

In this two-fold nihilism, both the human soul and the world are bereft of the plenitude of God's goodness and beauty. Human action, divorced from the compelling delight of God and God's good creation, is left with the "free choice" of an atomic and disintegrated self. *Acedia* thus reveals itself as ontological boredom, for the bored lack adequate desire, they sense that there is nothing worth desiring, which is precisely why the monk has hatred for his place, work, and life—goodness no longer delights:

It is the malaise of boredom . . . that is the full-flower of the voluntarism at the root of the culture of death, because it is boredom that finally completes voluntarism's nominalist project of denying the compulsion of transcendental beauty, goodness, and truth in the mediation of particular finite forms. In boredom, in our indifference to the vast array of numbingly indifferent choices, we see not only the . . . evacuation of finite form, but the evacuation of both the desire ordered to and dependent upon that form and the self-gift compelled by its claims upon our desire.[41]

In his Massey lectures originally titled *The Malaise of Modernity*, Charles Taylor proposes as an inescapable part of our personhood that we occupy moral space, the frameworks by which we orient our lives, values, decisions, understandings, and projects.[42] Moral

40. Hanby, "Boredom," 185.
41. Ibid., 187.
42. Taylor, *The Ethics of Authenticity*, 25.

space is "ontologically basic," and without it we would not even exist as human agents.[43] Agents without moral horizons are not free but rather without a sense of self or the ability to act rationally. We are not so sure about these frameworks anymore, aware that our own moral space, however constitutive of identity and however much it makes sense of world, is just one more form of life. We are, Taylor claims,

> never, or only rarely, really sure, free of all doubt, untroubled by some objection. . . . We live in a condition where we cannot help but be aware that there are a number of different construals, views which intelligent, reasonably undeluded people, of good will, can and do disagree on. We cannot help looking over our shoulder from time to time, looking sideways, living our faith also in a condition of doubt and uncertainty.[44]

Of course the change of the status of belief cannot but have effects, there must be "malaises."[45] Modern freedom occurs when older moral horizons were uprooted, when the great chain of Being was discredited, allowing us to "escape" the divine order. Free, yes, but the world also seems to have lost its magic, and we have experienced the "great disembedding," and have "a sense of malaise, emptiness, a need for meaning."[46] Corresponding to our freedom is the "mutual fragilization of all the different views" and the resultant "terrible flatness in the everyday," the "utter flatness, emptiness of the ordinary."[47] There is a sense that our freedom came at a cost, namely the loss of a higher purpose, of anything worth living for, and so the only remainder is a "centring on the self."[48] And since the world is devoid of thick meaning, the world itself loses depth, sinking to the level of mere resource for our use and abuse in pursuit of our own, rather shallow, comfort.[49]

---

43. Ibid.
44. Taylor, *A Secular Age*, 10–11.
45. MacIntyre, *After Virtue*, 71–72; Taylor, *The Ethics of Authenticity*, 1–12.
46. Taylor, *A Secular Age*, 302.
47. Ibid., 309.
48. Taylor, *The Ethics of Authenticity*, 4.
49. Ibid., 4–8.

Conclusion

Sloth hates our proper work, boredom refuses to will (through approving and loving the good) and nihilism is the noughting of the world and ourselves. But however distasteful, the slothful reject their own good, shuddering at their own cure, for fidelity—taking the yoke, the work God has given—is abhorrent, a cause of sadness. Sloth would rather be free than well.

In *The Unbearable Lightness of Being*, Milan Kundera gives us Tomas, an inveterate womanizer largely indifferent to the women he frequently seduces. Light and free, he hunts for some difference to distract from the boredom of it all. One of his conquests, the naive Tereza, comes to visit him in Prague and manages to spend the entire night with him, despite his attempts to evacuate her from his flat after their assignation. When he wakes, he discovers Tereza, still asleep, holding his hand: "Could they have been hand in hand all night? It was hard to believe."[50] He had never spent the night with a lover, as it was one of his cardinal rules that he "should exclude all love from his life."[51] And here she was, linking herself to him, clutching on, weighing him down, and "an aura of hitherto unknown happiness" finds him.[52] So much so that they both begin to look forward to sleeping together, sharing a bed and invariably holding hands; the narrator says, in a poignant line, that, "I might even say that the goal of their lovemaking was not so much pleasure as the sleep that followed it."[53] He is happy because he loses lightness, becomes heavy, and real. But is it worth it?

> The heaviest of burdens crushes us, we sink beneath it, it pins us to the ground. . . . The heavier the burden, the closer our lives come to the earth, the more real and truthful they become.
> Conversely, the absolute absence of a burden causes man to be lighter than air, to soar into the heights, take leave of the earth and

50. Milan Kundera, *The Unbearable Lightness of Being* (New York: Harper Perennial, 1991), 10.
51. Ibid., 13.
52. Ibid., 14.
53. Ibid., 14.

his earthly being, and become only half real, his movements as free as they are insignificant.

What then shall we choose? Weight or lightness?[54]

If we find freedom in this lightness of boredom, what shall we choose?

54. Ibid., 5.

4

Bleaching Things

In his theologically informed cookbook, Robert Farrar Capon provides an apologia for writing such a text even though an amateur cook, a mere lover:

> The world may not need another cookbook, but it needs all the lovers—amateurs—it can get. It is a gorgeous place, full of clownish graces and beautiful drolleries, and it has enough textures, tastes, and smells to keep us intrigued for more time than we have. Unfortunately, however, our response to its loveliness is not always delight: It is, far more often than it should be, boredom. And that is not only odd, it is tragic; for boredom is not neutral—it is the fertilizing principle of unloveliness.[1]

In the terrible state of boredom, "the man who thinks heedlessness a sin and boredom a heresy—is just the man you need."[2] For the lover, things are beautiful, sometimes even made beautiful as they "look the world back to grace," as opposed to the "boor" whose "boredom will break it to bits."[3] Consider a simple orange peel, suggests Capon, and notice it, this simple thing likely to be ignored and discarded; as "long as anyone looks at it in delight" it is like Eden, existing because "it is the orange peel hung on God's chandelier. . . . He likes it; therefore, it stays."[4] Without God's delight, we are noth-

---

1. Robert Farrar Capon, *The Supper of the Lamb: A Culinary Reflection* (New York: Macmillan, 1969), 3.

2. Ibid., 3–4.

3. Ibid., 4.

4. Ibid. See also Julian of Norwich, *Revelations of Divine Love*, trans. Clifton Wolters (New York: Penguin Books, 1966), 68: "It exists, both now and for ever, because God loves it. In short, everything owes its existence to the love of God."

ing, but we exist because of his infinite "yes" to us, and he give us work as a form of instruction to say "yes, at last" to ourselves, each other, and the things of the world, as he does.

The delight even of orange peels is found in M.F.K. Fisher. In France, newly married, with unpleasant lodgings, and alone for long stretches, she cooks tangerines on newspaper spread atop the radiator:

> My pleasure in them is subtle and voluptuous and quite inexplicable. . . . In the morning, in the soft sultry chamber, sit in the window peeling tangerines, three or four. Peel them gently; do not bruise them. . . . Listen to the chambermaid thumping up the pillows. . . . While she mutters of seduction and French bicyclists who ride more than wheels, tear delicately from the soft pile of sections each velvet string. You know those pulpy white strings that hold the tangerines to their skins? Tear them off. Be careful. . . . After you have put the pieces of tangerine on the paper on the hot radiator, it is best to forget about them. . . . On the radiator the sections of tangerines have grown even plumper, hot and full. You carry them to the window, pull it open, and leave them for a few minutes on the packed snow of the sill. They are ready. . . . I cannot tell you why they are so magical. Perhaps it is that little shell, thin as one layer of enamel on a Chinese bowl, that crackles so tinily, so ultimately under your teeth. Or the rush of cold pulp just after it. Or the perfume. I cannot tell.[5]

This little tangerine carries within it delight and goodness to those who love, to those not bored.

Boredom is a heresy, declaring God was wrong when he saw the goodness of the world. God "looks the world into loveliness," the bored think God's vision impaired. Whatever some think, we cannot be good Christians and despise the world, for to be "a Christian means a man who believes that deity or sanctity has attached to matter or entered the world of the senses."[6] Instead of despising the world, we are to love it passionately—amateurishly—into grace, for,

---

5. M.F.K. Fisher, *The Art of Eating* (Hoboken: Wiley Publishing, 2004), 26–28.

6. G.K. Chesterton, *Saint Thomas Aquinas* (New York: Image Books, 1956), 41–42.

like Chesterton says of Thomas Aquinas, it was "that positive position of his mind, which is filled and soaked as with sunshine with the warmth of the wonder of created things."[7] Or, as St. Augustine momentously discovered, everything God made was good and thus evil was no-thing; evil was a privation and deprivation of the good, but was no real thing.[8] Less abstractly, but in full agreement, are the famous lines of Belloc:

> Wherever the Catholic sun doth shine,
> There's always laughter and good red wine.
> At least I've always found it so.
> Benedicamus Domino![9]

A Session

At the risk of thinking too much of produce, return to Capon's amazing (and amazingly quirky) encounter with a simple onion. First, he instructs, we are to find three or four normal onions, selecting the best looking with which to spend sixty minutes of "excellent company"—although we must try, he exhorts us, to "firmly resist the temptation to feel silly."[10] Pulling up a chair, we are to address ourselves to the onion, noting, above all, "that the onion is a thing, a being, just as you are" and thus the confrontation between onion, person, knife, board, and chair constitutes "a place in the highest sense of the word. This is a Session, a meeting, a society of things."[11]

Capon continues to detail the glorious materiality of the onion—its lines, colors, texture, smell—cutting and dicing as small as he can before pressing and rolling it with fingers until it "yields all the water" it has and "is all but gone."[12] It is reduced to nothing but has revealed the deepest truth of all, which is that beneath its sheer con-

7. Ibid., 119.
8. Augustine, *Confessions*, trans. Henry Chadwick (New York: Oxford University Press, 1991), esp. Book 7.
9. Hilaire Belloc, "The Catholic Sun," Poemhunter.com, http://www.poemhunter.com/poem/the-catholic-sun-2/ (accessed July 15, 2014).
10. Capon, *Supper of the Lamb*, 11.
11. Ibid.
12. Ibid., 16.

tingency "lies the Act by which it exists" and which brings forth onions; "He likes onions, therefore they are."[13]

What of this interesting idea of the meeting of things, the session? Historically, a session indicated the meeting of a court or parliament, the gathering or sitting of an assembly, the meeting of a body endowed with some authority. In such an assembly, the members must recognize each other as having the prerogative to join, just as the whole assembly must be recognized as having some authority or jurisdiction to hear or try a case.[14] To note a session among the mutual confrontation of kitchen things and onions, then, requires recognizing the weight of its members.

According to Kenneth Schmitz, our older understanding of things conveys this sense of weight or importance, noting an "emphatic meaning of the word 'thing'" as an individual "distinguished from the totality of being," as well as "an assembly, a public meeting of some moment."[15] Linking the two meanings, "the word 'thing' often carries with it a certain self-assertiveness, a certain consistency and weight (according to the emphatic meaning), and also a certain importance and value (implied in the assembly meaning)."[16] Things, in this sense, bear interiority which they present or give to the world, and in that interiority possess a thickness, a weighty dignity which we ought to recognize and respect.

As examined earlier, this dignity is bequeathed to things by the creative gift of God, for things are given to themselves, but this very contingency establishes rather than diminishes their integrity and weight. In love, God chose to create and sustain them, and as creatures things bear the stamp of divine approval (willing in love). Thus the Catholic understanding of the worth of things goes far beyond the already elevated recognition of form and finality discernible to ancient philosophy, for things are more than self-governed unities with an internal source of stability and direction, as there is a genuinely "originating and communicating cause of

13. Ibid., 17.
14. Schmitz, *Recovery of Wonder*, 9.
15. Ibid.
16. Ibid.

being"—God—who gives this stability.[17] As genuinely communicative, and as really transcendent and thus without competition, God grants them the integrity of their own goodness, both recognizing and delighting in the being, agency, self-governance, and goodness of those things—He sees and approves of their goodness. (What sort of deity reserves all goodness to itself or is jealous of the good of another?) Consequently, in the medieval "understanding of things, all things, including physical things . . . there is a great, even infinite depth present within them" since God still "must dwell within them, sustain them every moment of their own existence."[18] Without reducing things to himself, God is immanent in them as their constant cause, giving them to themselves, closer to them than they are to themselves. Things, as such, while entirely themselves, are never just themselves.

Perhaps no one articulates this as powerfully as Gerard Manley Hopkins. In "As Kingfishers Catch Fire," for instance, he states the sheer, unrepeatable, thingness of things; each possessing its own act of being-given existence (*haeccitas*), an ongoing, dynamic making present, a presence-ing, a be-ing, a give-ing:

> … … … like each tucked string tells, each hung bell's
> Bow swung finds tongue to fling out broad its name;
> Each mortal thing does one thing and the same:
> Deals out that being indoors each one dwells;
> Selves; goes itself; *myself* it speaks and spells,
> Crying Whát I dó is me: for that I came.
> … Acts in God's eye what in God's eye he is—
> Christ—for Christ plays in ten thousand places,
> Lovely in limbs, and lovely in eyes not his
> To the Father through the features of men's faces.[19]

Each and every mortal thing communicates its interiority, flinging out the hidden mystery of its being, at the same time speaking forth Christ, through whom all things were made, in whom all things are

---

17. Ibid., 46.
18. Ibid.
19. Gerard Manley Hopkins, "As Kingfishers Catch Fire," *The Major Works*, ed. Catherine Phillips (New York: Oxford University Press, 2009), 129.

redeemed, and with whom all things utter back their joyous praise to the Father who loves (willing/unlacing/approving) them: "All things counter, original, spare, strange/...He fathers-forth whose beauty is past change:/Praise him."[20]

While entirely itself, no thing is merely itself, but is also the place of Christ, an assembly, and thus a glorious weight. The Hebrew "word for the glory of God (*kâbôd*) also carries with it the sense of weight," a weight immanently present at the core of all things:[21]

The world is charged with the grandeur of God.
It will flame out, like shining from shook foil;
...nature is never spent,
   There lives the dearest freshness deep down things;
And though the last lights off the black West went
   Oh, morning, at the brown brink eastward, springs—
Because the Holy Ghost over the bent
   World broods with warm breast and with ah! bright wings.[22]

Nature is rich, never spent, because deep down, at its innermost self, where most itself (for persons, their solitude) lies "received generosity," the grandeur and glory of God: no contradiction, no tension, no zero-sum between God and his creation, but self-communication, a pouring forth of generosity.[23] So generous as to approve of the weight (glory) of those things which God wills into existence: the glory of God is the person fully alive—*Gloria Dei vivens homo!*[24] Things have interiority, a depth and weight within them, and the fullness of (God's) being is present to them "without displacing them in any way."[25]

Given this fullness, as things present themselves—and recall that the core of being is self-communicative act seeking to operate or give itself—there is "an 'overflow' of presence" or "radiance" of being,

20. Gerard Manley Hopkins, "Pied Beauty," *The Major Works*, 132–33.
21. Schmitz, *Recovery of Wonder*, 47.
22. Gerard Manley Hopkins, "God's Grandeur," *The Major Works*, ed. Catherine Phillips (New York: Oxford University Press, 2009), 128.
23. Schmitz, *Recovery of Wonder*, 31.
24. John Paul II, *Evangelium Vitae*, 34, referencing St. Irenaeus.
25. Schmitz, *Recovery of Wonder*, 48.

Bleaching Things

what we could call the "*splendor formae*, 'splendour of form'. . . ."[26] If true, and if justice requires rendering things their due, then there is a kind of justice due to things, an "interior bond" shared by the whole community of being to not only recognize integrity but also delight in it, wonder at it, will it in the sense of approving its goodness. Formed and enlightened by love, our intelligence draws near the world in a kind of active receptivity—active because we are intelligent, active as in Adam's loving decision to delight in Eve, active like God's seeing and approving of the world's goodness; receptive because the world's things have their splendor as gift.[27] In love, we recognize the "authentic otherness" of things, not merely in their facticity or being-there, but in the beauty and goodness possessed by the thing as its own, now attended to and delighted in by us.[28]

As intelligent, we should approach the world with wonder, with deep amazement at the freshness deep down things, at the glorious weight they hold. Or, as Kenneth Schmitz puts it, we should attend to things methodically. Method is a seeking after something. In its linguistic origins it has similarity to the hunt, the attempt to capture or attain some desired end, and this hunt uses particular tools, the organon of reason and inquiry. A method, then, is a seeking after knowledge using the tools of intelligence. This is not a value-free activity which admits equally of any desired end using any possible tool, but, instead, resembles something like the good farmer who uses tools appropriate to the integrity of the land for the sake of a fruitful harvest, harming neither the fecundity of the land nor the well-being of the farmer: "the concept of method (*met'hodos*) is not simply a mental exercise but a way of life seeking the human and the universal good."[29]

This method, the life of theory, *bios thêoretikos*, is not essentially a life of abstraction but rather a life of attunement or attention to the real:

26. Rowan Williams, *Grace and Necessity: Reflections on Art and Love* (Harrisburg: Morehouse, 2005), 13.
27. George Grant, "Faith and the Multiversity." *Communio* 40 (Spring 2013): 161–196, at 163, 174.
28. Ibid., 164.
29. Schmitz, *Recovery of Wonder*, 14.

81

theory is openness to the things we have not made, the "unmake-
able things." It should be said, however, that by extension the theoretical attitude can be brought to all things, including artifacts,
since the emphasis of the *Bios thêoretikos* is upon fidelity to what is
observed, whether made by us or not . . . the original meaning of
theory is openness to the things that are . . . the heightened sensi-
bility with which we must dispose ourselves in order to receive
what others, including things, have to show to us.[30]

Theory, then, is fidelity to attending, an attunement to living in the
truth of being. Working with respect to the integrity of things is
work which attends, or, as we mean it here, theoretical work. Attunement to the glory of things is the methodical life of theory, a per-
petual openness, an active receptivity, the way of approval.

Inverting Theory

Bearing infinite weight, things possess their own interiority and
integrity and so they were understood by the medievals to be subjects rather than mere objects of being.[31] Not so for the moderns,
however, who reduced things to mere objects with extension. Flat-
tening and thinning things to matter in space, objects were stripped
of their glory. Moreover, a divide was imposed between the subjectivity of human consciousness and the objects standing against the
mind:

what is given in the modern paradigm is the project of reason to
gain objective knowledge. What is meant by objective? Object
means literally some thing that we have thrown over against ourselves. *Jacio* I throw, *ob* over against; therefore "the thrown
against." The German word for object is *Gegenstand*—that which
stands against. Reason as project . . . is the summonsing of something before us and the putting of questions to it, so that it is
forced to give its reasons for being the way it is an object.[32]

30. Ibid., 23.
31. Ibid., xiii.
32. Grant, "Faith and the Multiversity," 162.

Such summonsing reduces things to objects, envisioning objects as standing over there, bereft of purpose or splendor until summoned by us to serve our particular purpose. Rather than the attunement of wonder or love, the modern theoretical project, as against the radical openness of the older theoria, "would submit it to torture and in a wracking inquisition extract" answers from it.[33] The thing's authentic otherness is obscured, for when objects are forced to stand over against us before submitting to us, their interiority, goodness, and beauty are vacated: "But if we confine our attention to any thing as if it were simply an object, it cannot be loved as beautiful."[34] Objects become beautiful if they please us, according to our subjective taste, rather than demanding our delight as a matter of justice; objects become good if they serve us, according to our subjective purposes, rather than demand our willing them in keeping with God's own judgment and instruction.

For us, the world becomes mere resource, raw material, what Martin Heidegger called "standing-reserve," a stocking or storehouse of energy for us to use when and how we wish, waiting at attention for us.[35] Its interiority is denied, its *splendor formae* dimmed, and there is no *kâbôd* or "freshness deep down"; the Holy Ghost does not brood, Christ's play has stilled, and only we father forth. There are no gods anywhere, and the world has been stripped of its intrinsic value, serving at our beck and call. It is no longer gift, merely a stark given, mute:

> What are the roots that clutch, what branches grow
> Out of this stony rubbish? Son of man,
> You cannot say, or guess, for you know only
> A heap of broken images, where the sun beats,

33. Ratzinger, *In the Beginning*, 35; cf. Immanuel Kant, *Critique of Pure Reason*, trans. Werner S. Pluhar (Indianapolis: Hackett, 1996), 21: "When approaching nature, reason must . . . do so not in the capacity of a pupil who lets the teacher tell him whatever the teacher wants, but in the capacity of an appointed judge who compels the witnesses to answer the questions that he puts to them."
34. Grant, "Faith and the Multiversity," 166.
35. Martin Heidegger, *Basic Writings*, ed. David Farrell Krell (New York: HarperSanFrancisco, 1993), 322.

And the dead tree gives no shelter, the cricket no relief,
And the dry stone no sound of water.[36]

Further, any notion of being for the dirt, of keeping its integrity echoes very faintly in modern objectivity. Freedom "loses its hold on being," becomes unmoored, and refuses to recognize legitimate action as "exercised within the community of beings."[37] Freedom becomes superiority, an act of agency against the world, a declaration of emancipation from membership in the assembly. No longer will we allow ourselves to be addressed by the session of being, and no longer will we consider our freedom to be that of guards of the earth, tending and keeping that which is not ours, but for which we have responsibility, in order to offer all our works—including the work of our own selfhood—as provisions to fill the cosmic temple of our Master. Freedom, for those with *acedia*, is not recognized as a loving approval of the world, an at-tending and husbandry of its integral goodness in a way which develops or improves it: "The new freedom . . . is no longer an appetite for the other as embodying its good, but the affirmation of itself as its own good. Such freedom thus becomes a self-sustaining mode of life."[38]

Goodness without Truth

The Western tradition has long grappled with the question of freedom within the limits of natural right and natural law, a distinction vital to so much of our understanding of the rule of law, human dignity, and the meaning of human freedom and responsibility. If right is determined only by what we arbitrarily choose, then right is fundamentally unstable; but if there is a natural right, then justice is beyond mere caprice or accident but normative and binding. The explanation of how things were right by nature took many forms, and the West exists as the tension between the explanations offered by Jerusalem, Athens, and Rome. By the time of early modernity,

36. T. S. Eliot, *The Waste Land and Other Poems* (San Diego: Harvest, 1962), lines 19–24.
37. Schmitz, *Recovery of Wonder*, 79, 91.
38. Ibid., 98.

however, a new consensus emerged that nature (or creation) did not provide an explanation of the good. John Locke, for example, rejected the "old view of nature" and the understanding that "human beings were ... directed to a highest good under which all goods could be known in a hierarchy of subordination and superordination"—there simply was no such good.[39] In the absence of a normative ordering of goods, it became difficult, but essential, to explain the meaning and foundations of justice, and Locke and the liberal tradition declared that justice was contractual rather than rooted in nature. As George Grant articulates it, the fathers of modernity knew that their version of justice required "giving up the doctrine of creation as the primal teaching," for if there was truth "deep down things," if things were heavy in their interiority and made demands on us to be respected in their integrity, and if we were charged to work, tend, fill, and keep the garden through good work, offering both the perfected garden and our work-perfected selves as adornments for God's cosmic temple, then our contractual agreements were bound rather than free-floating.[40] More succinctly, if there was a truth about the good, then we were not entirely free to make justice in the image of our own unfettered wills; we were not sovereign, not autonomous, but remained ruled rulers. Modernity chafed on these limits, viewed them as obeisance rather than freedom, and determined that humanity "depends for its progress not on God or nature but on its own freedom, and the direction of that progress is determined" by our own self-understandings, although it is unclear whether those self-understandings can secure anything like the common good.[41]

As Grant sees it, in the "heartlands of ... empire" in which we find ourselves, the alienation from creation coupled with technological prowess and ill-defined freedom is self-destructive: "technology is now increasingly directed towards the mastery of human beings ... technology organizes a system which requires a massive

---

39. George Grant, *English-Speaking Justice* (Toronto: Anansi, 1985), 17.
40. Ibid., 19.
41. Ibid., 24.

apparatus of artisans concerned with the control of human beings. Such work as behavior modification, genetic engineering, population control by abortion are extreme examples."[42] Thus, our "exalted human freedom ... now threatens freedom," a phenomenon John Paul II notes:[43]

> with the new prospects opened up by scientific and technological progress there arise new forms of attacks on the dignity of the human being. At the same time a new cultural climate is developing and taking hold, which gives crimes against life a new and-if possible-even more sinister character, giving rise to further grave concern: broad sectors of public opinion justify certain crimes against life in the name of the rights of individual freedom, and on this basis they claim not only exemption from punishment but even authorization by the State, so that these things can be done with total freedom. . . .[44]

John Paul II taught repeatedly that certain "crimes against life" would be justified "in the name of the rights of individual freedom."[45] This system of rights-enshrined crime destroys itself—and becomes a factor leading to the destruction of others—when it no longer recognizes and respects its essential link with the truth. When such misunderstood autonomy governs our life, it is inevitable that others must be rejected, for "everyone else is considered an enemy from whom one has to defend oneself," since every other person is a competitor to our own unchecked sovereignty.[46] The common good is not sought, merely the individual good, and when goods conflict a breakdown of "genuinely human co-existence ... has already begun."[47]

Left unchecked by creation and governed by will, this terrible covenant of sloth, in all its bored nihilism, refuses to willingly approve or love reality—heedless of God's instruction to Adam, the

42. Ibid., 9.
43. Ibid., 10.
44. John Paul II, *Evangelium Vitae*, 4.
45. Ibid., 5.
46. Ibid., 20.
47. Ibid.

empire of desire looks at the assembly of being, the session of onions and persons and tackle and trim, and chooses not to say "At last," seeing nothing of value. The pleasure of membership in the grand communion of being has departed, leaving only our slothful abhorrence and sadness. There has been a "bleaching out of the density of things, of their depth and internal constitution," and a "lifting [of] the weight attributed to them."[48]

Contraception: An Excursus on the Empire of Death

One could hardly ask for a better example of the lifting of the proper weight attached to creation than our culture's use and understanding of contraception, especially as it rejects the health and well-being of the community of being. By health, says Wendell Berry, "we mean merely the absence of disease," whereas health is best understood as "wholeness."[49] Absent the surrounding folds of wholeness, we understand health in a fragmented, piecemeal fashion, without attention to the connectedness of body to soul, person to person, persons to creation. (99–102) To view health in isolation, as specialists tend, is to "collaborate in the destruction of the body. Healing is impossible in loneliness . . . To be healed we must come with all the other creatures to the feast of Creation." (99) Specializing in the body without consideration for the soul, or, for that matter, specializing in the soul without including the body in the health of the person, devalues the body, our own as well as the bodies of others:

> Contempt for the body is invariably manifested in contempt for other bodies—the bodies of slaves, laborers, women, animals, plants, the earth itself. Relationships with all other creatures become competitive and exploitive rather than collaborative and convivial. The world is seen and dealt with, not as an ecological

48. Schmitz, *Recovery of Wonder*, 80–85.
49. Wendell Berry, *The Art of the Commonplace: The Agrarian Essays of Wendell Berry*, ed. Norman Wirzba (Washington, DC: Shoemaker and Hoard, 2002), 98. As this work is cited often in this chapter, hereafter page references will be given in parentheses following the quotation.

community, but as a stock exchange, the ethics of which are based on the tragically misnamed "law of the jungle"...body is thus sent to war against itself. (101)

In this mode of thinking, the other has no intrinsic relation to the self and must be understood in terms of opposition, as an object of competition, threat, or consumption: "We thus condemn ourselves to a loneliness for which the only compensation is violence—against other creatures, against ourselves." (102)

Our conception of sexuality is caught in our broader ecological and social disruption resulting in the "industrial phenomenon, in which the body is used as an idea of pleasure or a pleasure machine with the aim of 'freeing' natural pleasure from natural consequence." (75) So isolated from the end of fertility, sex suffers the "takeover by specialists . . . the sexual clinicians and the pornographers, both of whom subsist on the increasing possibility of sex between people who neither know nor care about each other . . . by separating it absolutely from the problems of fertility." (126–27) This is done in the name of "freedom," but by "'freeing' food and sex from worry, we have also set them apart from thought, responsibility, and the issue of quality." (129)

Sex without fertility is sex without much need for thought, ceding responsibility for sexuality to the specialists. Birth control becomes as carelessly added to the purchase list as any other commodity without concern for the total health of persons and culture. Further, this reduced sexuality loses its proper relationship to the household and the household economy, it becomes "'autonomous,' to be valued only for its own sake, therefore frivolous, therefore destructive. . . ." (112) Absent the context of the household and its concrete economy, sexual morality itself becomes commodified, for the body becomes property over which one has a right to use and exploit as one wishes. As a commodity, the rules of use are determined by the voluntary choice of the owner who posts either a sign of "Welcome" or "Keep Out/Private Property." (114) In this context, the arguments of even some traditionalists about the sanctity of marriage are somewhat misguided since they understand the body as property, just now co-owned by another contractually. Such a contract is simply the result of a free choice and carries no bonds other than the voluntariness of the agreement—still the capitalization of the body and its relationships.[50]

Berry, an agrarian, is concerned for the land, but his arguments are as much cultural as environmental, for environmental health cannot be understood without a wholeness including people and culture. Consequently, he criticizes the unthinking use of birth control because of its participation in a culture of commodification, violence, and isolation, considering only autonomous freedom rather than health. Thus, "birth control is a serious matter, both culturally and biologically" since it is part of a culture ignorant of its destructiveness. (129) He concludes:

> What is horrifying is not that we are relying so exclusively on a technology of birth control that is still experimental, but that we are using it casually, in utter cultural nakedness, unceremoniously, without sufficient understanding, and as a substitute for cultural solutions—exactly as we now employ the technology of land use. And to promote these means without cultural and ecological insight, as merely a way to divorce sexuality from fertility, pleasure from responsibility—or to sell them that way for ulterior "moral" motives—is to try to cure a disease by another disease. (129–130)

Berry has made an argument rooted in concerns for integrated wholeness—health—suggesting such health is recognized best by those formed in love:

> Like divine love, earthly love seeks plenitude; it longs for the full membership to be present and to be joined ... efficiency ignores both loves, earthly and divine, because by definition it must reduce experience to computation, particularity to abstraction, and mystery to a small comprehensibility. Efficiency, in our present sense of the world, allies itself inevitably with machinery. . . . (153–54)

Boredom, as explained earlier, concurs with Berry's claim that the cause of the "present age" of "disintegration and division, isolation and suffering" is a dualism which cannot see that "Creation is one

---

50. This is a particular problem for some Protestants influenced by a strain of voluntarism in Luther and Calvin. Emphasizing the sovereignty of God as the exercise of choice, command, or election, God is limited only by God's will rather than by the Trinitarian reality.

continuous fabric" and instead thinks of Creation as "divided into 'levels' that can readily be peeled apart. . . ." (145, 147) Specialization especially seems to understand reality as disintegrated and manipulable, just as the specialists of fertility and pornography understand sexuality. Rejecting the delight of the whole of goodness, all reality is open to our exploitation, equivalent to boredom.

Without the order of love, humans tend towards the "escapist pleasure of the consumer economy or the rapacious consensual exploitation which increasingly marks the human relationships formed by that economy."[51] The unthinking abuse of birth control, then, is part of an economy "obsessed with 'programming, controlling, and dominating birth and death,'"[52] divorced from the wholeness of Creation, the wholeness of the Other, and the wholeness of the self, since in this dominance-obsessed economy, "the other simply becomes an object of consumption, the apparatus necessary for me to 'love' myself. . . ."[53]

In the end, the unthinking use of contraception is best understood as part of a culture so inflicted with *acedia* that it destroys its own health. Obsessed with autonomy, this economy is willing to violate the integrity of reality to remove any natural consequences of aggressive but frustrated desire: "we find a whole series of products deprived of their malignant property: coffee without caffeine, cream without fat, beer without alcohol . . . virtual sex without sex."[54] Having dis-integrated acts and things from the health of creation, we free ourselves from the worry of the natural consequences of food and sex but render ourselves incapable of taking genuine delight in either.

Conclusion

As T.S. Eliot noted, "the nymphs are departed," the glory and weight of the disenchanted world is hard to see given the "gradual bleeding and bleaching out" of the sense that things possessed

---

51. Hanby, "Boredom," 193.
52. Ibid., 188, quoting John Paul II.
53. Ibid., 193.
54. Ibid., 186, n. 7, quoting Slavoj Zizek.

integrity, and that the purpose of our work included keeping the world, acting for the soil even as we perfected ourselves by developing it, filling the temple of God with good things which we had loved into being.[55] The wonder and deep amazement at the world is an offense, the freedom of birds a threat, and to the suzerains of sloth, everything must be made to stand at attention, awaiting our orders, or risk being scratched out by our terrible sadness, our refusal to will the world. Called to the wonders of *theoria*—"At last!"—we are bored, we look at the world and know nothing, see nothing, and remember nothing of value, for both we and it have become noughting, just as the noonday demon wishes.[56]

What to do? If taking the yoke cures sloth, which yoke?

---

55. Eliot, "Waste Land," line 175; Schmitz, *Recovery of Wonder*, 106–07.
56. Ibid., line 123.

Part Three

Lovely Resistance

5

Sabbath Work, Sabbath Feasting

Created in the self-communicative image of God, humans exist to offer themselves as gifts while joyously welcoming the gift of others. To help us accomplish this end, God instructs Adam, not only in the task of finding and welcoming a helper, but also through the work mandates, to work and keep, to govern, and to fill. Through good work both we and the world are perfected, made suitable adornments for God's own temple.

In its most basic form, good work wills or approves the goodness of the world, even while developing the world in keeping with its form and rhythm. The slothful, however, (1) abhor the real, (2) have a repugnance (sadness) at their own purpose, and (3) are incapable of acting in keeping with their own proper good, a profound self-contradiction and alienation. Unable to love the world or perform good work, the slothful are bored and nihilistic, seeing nothing compelling or delightful in reality or their own selves. In the end, they would rather be untethered and "free" than happy, rejecting anything which might prevent "man's true and divinized self from falling prey to forgetfulness" in a "decision in favor of . . . hatred for the divine in man."[1] Hating the work and reality God has given, the slothful choose instead a "light" freedom, willing to violate the integrity of any and every thing so long as they remain suzerains of their own weightless empire of desire.

An enchanted cosmos always speaks, however, flinging out the weight of glory deep down things. Created through the free love of God who declares it good, the world is charged with the grandeur of God; all that is has Christ immanently present while retaining its

---

1. Pieper, *Faith, Hope, Love*, 121.

own integrity and autonomy. The world is gifted and dependent, but with its own splendor of form, its own goodness. The bored cannot see—will not see—this goodness, perceiving the world as mere object in service of arbitrary whim and pleasure. Disenchanted, the world is bereft of loveliness to the slothful—and there are many afflicted by sloth in our own time, an epoch subjected to sloth's terrible covenant. For all that, though, there is a freshness deep down things. The world remains a gift of God, charged with the grandeur and *kâbôd* of the Trinitarian outpouring, and we remain workers tilling and filling the world with augmented goodness. If we embrace our place, sloth would be overcome and we would act as we were meant. Exorcising the noon day demon is not accomplished merely with the right ideas or worldview, though, since sloth is a stance toward the world, an attunement out of tune with the active receptivity of *theoria*. Judge Holden will not be cured by ideas alone, but by a therapy of his loves, by being put back in tune.

God's instruction is needed, and yet God often teaches through ordinary things, through things available if we would attend. Sabbath, I suggest, is one of those ordinary things already provided to instruct and cure our loves, and if we would keep Sabbath we would be on our way to singing of the world's loveliness.[2]

Celebration, the Opposite of Sloth

Although a misunderstanding, sloth is commonly defined as laziness or idleness cured with some hard work.[3] But sloth, as Josef Pieper reminds us: (1) lacks magnanimity and the courage to accept the great dignity to which God has called us;[4] (2) "does not wish to be what [it] really, fundamentally, is;"[5] and (3) perverts humility, rejecting our greatness because loathing friendship with God and

2. Josef Pieper, *Only the Lover Sings: Art and Contemplation*, trans. Lothar Krauth (San Francisco: Ignatius Press, 1990).

3. Pieper, *Faith, Hope, Love*, 118; cf. *Leisure the Basis of Culture*, trans. Alexander Dru (New York: Mentor-Omega, 1963), 38–39.

4. Pieper, *Faith, Hope, Love*, 119.

5. Pieper, *Leisure*, 38.

its concomitant obligations.[6] Consequently, the opposite of sloth is not industry but "man's . . . affirmation of his own being . . . which is to say love."[7] Sloth's opposite is to will (approve/love/affirm) our proper work and dignity.

Sloth is overcome when we affirm the goodness of the world, just as God does. Perhaps one could even understand the instruction of Adam in the naming of the animals and the gift of Eve as a primordial teaching on sloth. Already in a state of goodness, without original sin, it was possible for Adam to abhor the place given him, to feel sadness at the incredible dignity conferred. Given the staggering weight of the responsibility to develop the garden, Adam could have experienced his aloneness as an occasion for sadness; he could have willed it to be otherwise, longed for a life of lesser dignity, free to enjoy the wildness and lightness of the animals. In sloth, Adam could have abhorred the incredible good given to him, and eventually did so, willing something other than his own proper being.

Adam now needs to recover the will to act—to affirm his own being and to work in keeping with his responsibility. But a discordant will cannot simply will itself back into tune. Instruction is necessary, and not by ideas alone, for it is not merely our belief about ourselves which is slothful, although that too, but our stance, our way of dwelling in the world. We need to dwell differently, and this requires cultural forms and practices, not merely lectures and ideas—the "charge" at the heart of things needs attention.[8]

For this we require leisure. Not to be confused with spare-time or down-time, genuine leisure is not non-activity but "a mental and spiritual attitude"—an attunement—"not simply the result of external factors."[9] As a "condition of the soul," leisure is possible only when we acquiesce to our own being, confidently approving of the integrity and direction of the created nature of things.[10] Like *theoria*, leisure stands in radical openness to the real, with deep

---

6. Pieper, *Faith, Hope, Love*, 119–20.

7. Pieper, *Leisure*, 39.

8. Norman Wirzba, *Living the Sabbath: Discovering the Rhythms of Rest and Delight* (Grand Rapids: Brazos, 2006).

9. Ibid., 40.

10. Ibid., 40–41.

amazement and approval. At the root of good work lies contemplation, an attitude of "celebration."[11]

Too often, contemplation is presented as a withdrawal from the world into the enclosing reserve of one's own self, generally in a kind of stultifying silence. It is true that contemplation requires attentiveness, but contemplation steps away from the hustle not in withdrawal, and not as passivity, but as active receptivity, as an engagement reaching out to things with "loving acceptance" and "affectionate affirmation."[12] Not a shrinking back, but a recalibration, a making visible what had been overlooked, a recognition of goodness through love: "*ubi amor, ibi oculus*—the eyes see better when guided by love."[13]

Contemplation is not a passive indifference, not a stilling or cessation of activity, but a theoretical activity of particular intensity—a determined reaching out to the world in "expectant alertness."[14] It is a celebration drawing "vitality from affirmation."[15] Just as God ends his work in Genesis by affirming the goodness of that work, so contemplation actively celebrates: we look for goodness, we affirm goodness, we celebrate goodness. Nor should we think of this celebration as some recondite accomplishment of the mystic only. Not at all. Indeed, the highest "form of affirmation is the festival," and the true contemplative looks for the public and festive aspect of the world.[16]

The festival is impossible without contemplation. Not a vacation, but a day in which the usual bonds of servile work are loosed so as to allow activity meaningful in itself, free activity. Most tasks do not provide their own justification but are done for the sake of something else. Some unpleasant chore is undertaken because it "has to be done" or "for the money," and so the task is rendered servile,

11. Ibid., 42.

12. Pieper, *Only the Lover Sings*, 75.

13. Ibid., 74.

14. Pieper, *In Tune with the World: A Theory of Festivity*, trans. Richard and Clara Winston (South Bend: St. Augustine's Press, 1999), 17.

15. Pieper, *Leisure*, 42.

16. Ibid., 43; cf. *Only the Lover Sings*, 17, 69.

which is not to say unnecessary or undignified, but performed not for its own sake.[17]

Festivity serves no purpose and requires no justification beyond itself. There may be benefits from festivity, to be sure, such as letting off steam, social concord, health, and so on, but planning to bring about these goods would no longer allow festivity, which is why such events are usually distasteful or numbingly boring (in the first sense of situative boredom). A festival exists for no reason other than the festival.

In ordinary labor, we are concerned that the effort accomplishes its purpose. Toiling away at some task without accomplishment would be failure, perhaps pointless. In festivity, the whole notion of success or failure is irrelevant since one does not fail at feasting except by feasting in order to succeed at some other task: "concern for success or failure of an act falls away."[18] Insofar as one feasts to feast, one has "succeeded" at feasting. To be so careless, to expend effort and energy without success or payoff would be bizarre, even deeply foolish, if done every day. But festivity is free just insofar as we "work" while expecting nothing in return other than that action itself.

As pointless, or at least lacking some external return, festivity gives up the usual expectation of reward or yield or profit. It makes an offering of its labor, sacrificing without hope of return on the sacrifice. Such offering is possible only from a disposition of abundance, of wealth: "not, to be sure, the wealth of money, but of existential richness. Absence of calculation, in fact, lavishness, is one of its elements."[19] This can be done in a chaotic or irrational way, of course, but all festivity carries with it a "waste of yield," an "extravagance" surpassing the rules of instrumental rationality.[20] Lavishness does not violate reason, but makes sense given "an existential concord of man with the world and with himself" only if the world is seen as abundant, good, lovely, rich, and worth celebrating.[21]

17. Pieper, In Tune with the World, 7–12.
18. Ibid., 17.
19. Ibid., 19.
20. Ibid., 20.
21. Ibid., 21.

Thus, only the lover—the non-slothful—who wills/loves/approves the goodness of the world in comprehensive and ultimate affirmation can celebrate the festival. There are lots of parties (recall the second form of boredom), but festivity requires love: "'*Ubi caritas gaudet, ibi est festivas,*' 'Where love rejoices, there is festivity.'"[22] Celebration cannot occur without willing the world as God sees it, without loving its goodness; in fact, God's very nature is celebratory, an endless dance of mirth. Finding people capable of feasting is something of a challenge, then, for "whoever refuses assent to reality as a whole"—like the slothful, who are legion—"no matter how well off he may be, is by that fact incapacitated for either joy or festivity."[23] However much their material goods and pleasures, the "barren," are "unable to celebrate a feast," and even whole times can be barren.[24]

Instructing the Captives

Some are barren, slothfully incapable of feasting; if so, keeping Sabbath would be a challenge, even an impossibility, for us. Or, perhaps Sabbath is particularly given to the barren as a special instruction, a practice able to reorient and enliven slothful loves. Something similar occurs when God forms a people at Sinai, offering "this motley multitude of ex-slaves" formed in the patterns of bondage an invitation, and the necessary instruction, to become a new community with a new form of life.[25] Nor is this irrelevant to us, for while the covenant obviously acts to form a particular community, the text is introduced by identifying God as the speaker but without identifying the audience; we are told that "God spoke all these words" (Ex 20:1), but the address is not explicitly limited to those present at Sinai. Further, the injunctions are given to "you," to the whole assembly and to each person individually, so while spoken at a given

22. Ibid., 23.
23. Ibid., 26.
24. Pieper, *Only the Lover Sings*, 66.
25. Leon R. Kass, "The Ten Commandments: Why the Decalogue Matters," *Mosaic Magazine*, June 2013, http://mosaicmagazine.com/essay/2013/06/the-ten-commandments/.

time and place, "the content of the speech is not parochial" but universal, given "to anyone and everyone."[26]

As universal, the opening reminder that "I am the LORD your God, who brought you out of the land of Egypt, out of the house of bondage" (Ex 20:2), while indicating a historical event, speaks also of a universal human possibility, including our own bondage:

> The Lord appears to be suggesting that for the children of Israel—if not also for other unnamed auditors—there are basically two great alternatives: either to be in relation to the Lord, in Whose image humankind was created, or to be a slave to Pharaoh, a human king who rules as if he were himself divine. Egypt, identified redundantly as "the house of bondage," is presented here not just as one alternative among many but as the alternative to living as men and women whose freedom—from bondage not only to Pharaoh but to their own worst tendencies—seems to depend on embracing the covenant with the Lord.[27]

Bondage to our worst tendencies, including the possibility of rejecting the good offered by God, threatens us all. But just as God's instruction brings all out of Egypt, even those trapped by sloth can enter into freedom.

And in this "people-forming covenant," Sabbath stands out as one of only two commandments to receive a "positive exhortation," and is one of the longest instructions.[28] Also, it is the only one to give the direction to hallow or make holy. Sabbath, it would seem, is essential to escaping Egypt.

> Remember the Sabbath day, to keep it holy. Six days you shall labor, and do all your work; but the seventh day is a Sabbath to the LORD your God; in it you shall not do any work, you, or your son, or your daughter, your manservant, or your maidservant, or your cattle, or the sojourner who is within your gates; for in six days the LORD made heaven and earth, the sea, and all that is in them, and rested the seventh day; therefore the LORD blessed the Sabbath day and hallowed it (Ex 20:8–11).

26. Ibid.
27. Ibid.
28. Ibid.

Oddly, however, in its demand to "remember," the commandment seems to assume that the Israelites already had experienced Sabbath. How would they?

Leon Kass suggests the provision and rules of manna provide helpful context.[29] Having left the relatively well-fed slavery of Egypt behind for the bare subsistence of desert freedom, the people remember with some fondness the comforts of their former position, prompting God to provide manna from heaven, enough for all, although they are not to gather more than they can use or store any for the next day, with the exception of the double portion on the sixth day since no manna would appear on the seventh. With this cycle of provision and rest, God instructs the people that his creation is not one of scarcity but abundance, not competition but gratitude, and things are fundamentally ordered in such a way that "one may—one should—regularly desist from acquiring and provisioning, in an expression of trust, appreciation, and gratitude for the world's bounty."[30]

Manna trains a festive disposition, for only a grasp of existential richness and extravagance allows festivity. And here we find God creating a pattern and rhythm of work and rest linked to his abundant generosity. When God makes good (things) appear from heaven, then asks his people to trust that it will reappear tomorrow, even in the midst of the desert, forbidding any attempt to seek security, he wants his people to know him as inexhaustibly generous, particularly in distinction to the competition and inequities of Egypt.

While the restatement of the commands in Deuteronomy explicitly recalls deliverance from Egypt (Deut 5:15), Exodus commands remembrance of Sabbath, even though God is explicitly telling them of it for the first time: "Remember the Sabbath . . . for in six days the LORD made heaven and earth . . . and rested the seventh day." In remembering his own work and rest, God invites Israel "symbolically to relive it."[31] In doing so, the people are called to

29. Ibid.
30. Ibid.
31. Ibid.

remember and imitate the creator, to be like God. Not only does "inviting and requiring all members of the community to imitate the divine" teach "the radical equality of human beings," including the value of servants and animals, but also lifts our aspirations and concerns beyond the scrabbling of survival, suggesting our profound dignity.[32] In Egypt, where "men do not know or acknowledge the bountiful and blessed character of the given world," God's people fall prey to the worship of power and the abuse of each other, but Sabbath "promotes internal freedom ... by moderating" our passions, teaching the fundamental goodness of the world, even fostering a "truly humanistic politics" of dignity and equality.[33]

Linking Sabbath to the making present of creation, including the gratuitous abundance and goodness of God's work, is emphasized when God asks Israel (Deut 5:12) to guard the Sabbath.[34] This language suggests the keeping mandate of Genesis 2:15, where the task of guarding was not limited to one day alone but was universal. A similar comprehensiveness of Sabbath is emphasized in that the hallowing (*qadesh*), or setting apart, of the Sabbath indicated no "special object, place, or practice" but rather time and its use, leaving six days for human concerns and a seventh reserved to God:

> remembering it can and should take place all week long, reconfiguring out perception of time and its meaning. Under this radically new understanding the six days of work and labor point toward and are completed by the seventh day and its hallowing. Mindfulness of sanctified time makes an edifying difference ... all the time.[35]

Every day of work is positioned within a remembrance of Sabbath, last week's and the one yet to come, and places servile work in the context of an activity meaningful in itself—a festival—even as Sabbath points to the original work in the garden. This day of work,

32. Ibid.
33. Ibid.
34. Ibid.
35. Ibid; cf. Abraham Joshua Heschel, *The Sabbath* (New York: Farrar, Straus and Giroux, 1951), 6–10.

that particular task, is narrated within a story of creation and Sabbath rest, within a call to be like God, and within mandates to work, tend, keep, and fill the garden. All work references Sabbath.

Working on Sabbath

We are to guard Sabbath as we are to guard the garden, but while we are to work the garden, Sabbath is a time of rest, an absence of work. Or so we often think. It is not really quite so simple. One of the most interesting aspects of Sabbath, both in the Decalogue and in the creation account, is its hallowing (*qadosh/kadosh*) of time rather than place. The mythical mind tends to declare sites as the origin of the world or the residence of God (the navel, *omphalos*), setting aside mountains or groves for that purpose, but in Hebrew Scripture there

> is a radical departure from accustomed religious thinking. The mythical mind would expect that, after heaven and earth have been established, God would create a holy place—a holy mountain or a holy spring—whereupon a sanctuary is to be established. Yet it seems as if to the Bible it is holiness in time, the Sabbath, which comes first.[36]

As an experience and hallowing of time, Sabbath allows a making holy of all life in a way that a sanctified space may not. If this space is holy, then that place is non-holy, either profane or even unholy, and the clear demarcations allowed by sight tends to reify the difference. Take a small blue square set inside of a much larger white square. As you see them, each is present by relating to each other in their difference, each is first present by not being the other.

Of course, space need not be conceived this way, but it tends that way, particularly because sight/space is "par excellence the sense of the simultaneous"—something is present here but absent there.[37] Hearing differs, though, in providing "only dynamic and never static reality," like hearing a song which is never present all at once

36. Heschel, *The Sabbath*, 9, 95–96.
37. Hans Jonas, in Snell, *Through a Glass Darkly*, 17.

but always recedes to make way for the next sounds.[38] Songs are unified in our memory of the experience, not in the presentation of the sound. Memory unifies multiple times, and times are never merely simultaneous.

Calling us to remember Sabbath in the Decalogue, God calls us to relive or make present something of his original hallowing when he rests from his own work. In a similar way, the anamnesis or remembering of the Eucharist makes present a past event—the crucifixion—even as we recall the Last Supper and anticipate the Wedding Feast of the Lamb. As a sacrament, many things are signified, including "a reminder of the past . . . and [an] indication of that which is effected in us . . . and a prognostic, that is, a foretelling of future glory."[39] Like this, Sabbath calls us to guard and remember a time; moreover, a time unrelated to natural phenomena like new moons or lunar crescents but defined entirely by the act of God.[40]

Remembering, we make present or participate in God's own hallowing of creation. We should notice the activity, for remembering is not passive, not a relaxation or easing of our energy, but an act, a making present of God's activity. Sabbath is not the absence of work or idling away of time to enable work again the next day: "Sabbath . . . is not for the purpose of recovering one's lost strength and becoming fit for the forthcoming labor," not a prudential means to "enhancing the efficiency of [our] work."[41] Sabbath is "not for the sake of the weekdays," and is not a respite from real life "but the climax of living."[42] Sabbath's placement on the final day of creation indicates its priority; "last in creation, first in intention," "the end of the creation of heaven and earth."[43] The six days of work point to, serve, and derive their meaning from Sabbath, even as they become sanctified in themselves by the anamnesis, or making present, of Sabbath, which is not a mere thinking about but an "actively making real."

38. Ibid.
39. Aquinas, *ST* III. 60. 3.
40. Heschel, *The Sabbath*, 10.
41. Ibid., 14.
42. Ibid.
43. Ibid.

Lest this talk of the activity of Sabbath seem counter to the restful spirit of the day, recall that God very much acts on the seventh day:

> Thus the heavens and the earth were finished, and all the host of them. And on the seventh day God finished his work which he had done, and he rested on the seventh day from all his work which he had done. So God blessed the seventh day and hallowed it, because on it God rested from all his work which he had done in creation (Gen 2:1–3).

Not only does God bless and hallow the day, but it is on the seventh day, not the sixth, that creation is finished. The image of God working for six days and then not working on the seventh is not quite right; he works for six, forming and filling, before finishing his work on the seventh.[44] What was lacking? What did God need to bring about to finish his work? "Obviously," says Heschel, "there was an act of creation on the seventh day," for just as "heaven and earth were created in six days, *menuha* [rest] was created on the Sabbath."[45]

Just as heaven and earth were created through God's act, so too did God create on the Sabbath—"the work on weekdays and the rest on the seventh day are correlated"—to bring about something that was lacking, for the earth's formless void was not yet filled.[46] While *menuha* is generally translated as rest, it is not a negation but "something real and intrinsically positive," for without it the universe would not be finished.[47] *Menuha* is peace, tranquility, harmony, happiness, beatitude, and praise.

As first in intention, all creation "is oriented to Sabbath . . . it is oriented to worship" and praise, and creation "fulfills its purpose and assumes its significance when it is lived . . . with a view to worship."[48] In the "freedom of worship," the human "participates in

---

44. In the Vulgate, *conplevitque*, or ended/finished, is used in Gen 2:2, and also in 2 Chronicles 7:11 when Solomon finished the temple and palace, a fitting image for the building and provisioning imagery discussed in Chapter 2.

45. Ibid., 22.

46. Ibid.

47. Ibid., 22–23.

48. Ratzinger, *In the Beginning*, 27; *Catechism of the Catholic Church*, sec. 347.

God's freedom, in God's rest, and thus in God's peace."[49] That is, worship, as a free act like God's own, is meaningful itself, serving no ulterior purpose. Sabbath, like festival, is good per se and not for its benefits, and it is offered only to the "free children of God" as a mark and fulfillment of their deep dignity which is that God "pour[s] out his love upon us and . . . invite[s] us to love him in return."[50] Sabbath is an act of love for what "man . . . and God have in common,"[51] namely, self-communicative love.

The seventh day, like any feast, reveals the existential richness at the heart of the world, understood by Christians as the infinite dance of generosity, which is the Godhead, and the endless out-pouring of that generosity to the world, including the extravagant act of making humans with such dignity that we can, like God, give of ourselves with disregard for the external benefits of doing so—even though such giving is our purpose, fulfillment, and full act or rest (*menuha*). In guarding Sabbath, we guard all of creation, for only a people instructed or trained to see and celebrate abundant richness can approach the rest of their lives, the other six days and the work of those days, with a festive eye.

Sabbath teaches us to guard everything—to respect the integrity of things—by making us festive people, the non-barren capable of noting and attending to the richness deep down things. Sabbath rejects sloth, in other words, and Sabbath-time redeems all time as we grasp the orientation of all things to worship. If we are to see all the world as God sees it—as Christ playing in ten thousand places—we must know the pouring forth of divine play in creation and the making of menuha, the rest of fully communicative act. Only those celebrating the great feast say "At last!" about anything.

Sabbath Work

If we understand our instructions to fill, govern, tend, and keep the garden as comprehensive and related mandates rather than isolated

---

49. Ibid., 30–31.
50. Ibid., 30.
51. Heschel, *The Sabbath*, 15.

and reductionistic commands, we can begin to think of Sabbath
work as an aspiration or guide for all of human life. As I've suggested earlier, God instructs humans through the "test" of finding a
helper and in the creation mandates, trying to help us understand
(1) our own status as subjects, created in the image of God and
endowed with the dignity of conferring gift; (2) the responsibility to
see the goodness of things as God sees goodness; and (3) that all our
life and actions and work exist primarily for their subjective end
even as they develop the objective good(s) of the world.

That last sentence is inadequate. Yes, work serves its subjective
end even as developing the objective good(s) of the world, but we
might replace even as with inasmuch as, for any work trampling the
integrity of things, pattern, or direction violates the value of persons. Slothful work violates the goodness of the world and the
responsibility to keep the logic and rhythm of the world, thereby
refusing the dignity of our human vocation. It is not as though we
can violate the world and its things and embrace our own perfection as subjects and selves. Freedom without truth, the terrible covenant of Judge Holden, brings no good to Holden as a person, even
if he consents and chooses such weightless freedom. Human persons flourishes if—and only if—they bear *kâbôd*, if they act what in
God's eye they are.

Against sloth we have Sabbath work, work such as God did on
the seventh day. Of course there is a call to rest on the Sabbath, but
that command elevates and sanctifies all good work, even unpleasant and toilsome drudgery (*bonum arduum*), offered as worship by
those with festive hearts. Any good work can be sanctified, and any
sanctified work perfects us. As God teaches us festivity, he makes
possible our own co-redemptive work, if we would but work well.

Sabbath or festive work can be a source of celebration. Work
done in the well-fed "fleshpots" of symbolic Egypt, with its perennial tendency to exploitation, looks always to destroy and reduce
everything to mere resource, turning the world and all its inhabit-
ants—persons, too—into standing reserve. Such bored nihilism has
no real pleasure, for in its stance everything is "noughting," bearing
no weight or glory or value, unable to captivate. For the bored,
work and its "goods" are mere distractions, the acts of those who

hate their place and task, who feel only sadness at their own dignity and responsibility, and who have a deep aversion to good acts. Their work is ugly, and their working is without delight. Good work, on the other hand, is pleasant: "Where is our comfort but in the free, uninvolved, finally mysterious beauty and grace of this world that we did not make, that has no price?"[52]

Wendell Berry recounts a day with his young granddaughter hauling loads of dirt—with hand tools and horse cart—while cleaning the barn. Hard work, this: physically demanding, perhaps not entirely without smell and sweat. Yet, as she recognizes with pride her own performance, joining her efforts in service of family, place, and soil, she finds satisfaction and companionship. During one long silence, during which Berry was afraid she "was not saying anything because she was cold and tired and miserable and perhaps homesick," she leans to him and says "Wendell, isn't it fun?"[53]

It is not always fun, exactly, as any worker knows, but it can be good. Sabbath work continues God's own Sabbath work of finishing creation by filling the cosmic temple with good things, which we do by looking the world to grace through our own love, a love which sees and delights in the goodness deep down things.

52. Berry, *Commonplace*, 215.
53. Ibid., 218.

6

Small is Beautiful

It is sometimes thought that sanctity requires stubbing out certain aspects of our nature, excising parts of our personality or powers. This is not really Christian, however, for there "is nothing, no substance, no power, no faculty, in man that is in itself bad."[1] Sin impairs but does not destroy our nature; furthermore, in the Incarnation, "our Lord assumed our nature in its entirety, and ... whatever belongs to our nature was in Him," and since he cannot enter into union with anything inherently evil, there is nothing of our nature itself which is evil per se.[2] Ontologically, our nature is and remains good. Of course, Christianity recognizes moral evil, and the disorder of sin deadens and perverts everything, but, still, sanctity requires not that "men ... crush and kill their powers, but ... find their true use and to use them ... holiness is not the emptying of life, but the filling."[3]

Consequently, holiness never merely roots out vice but develops virtue. Merely removing vice leaves an emptiness, but the saints are full, youthful, lacking nothing human. Holiness requires "not to destroy ... or rid ... anything inherent" to humanity, but to "use it, weakened and debased as it is, in the energetic choice of good."[4] It is not God's nature to decrease, and as the Father's fullness remains even when giving to the Son, so the Son is undiminished by giving to us. He has no need to take away or destroy our humanity: "He

---

1. B. W. Maturin, *Self-Knowledge and Self-Discipline* (1909; reprt. n.p. Forgotten Books, 2012), 51.
2. Ibid.
3. Ibid., 52–53.
4. Ibid., 55.

himself is life, and light, and truth, not keeping within himself the wealth of these blessings, but pouring it forth upon all others, and even after the outpouring still remaining full. He suffers loss in no way by giving his wealth to others, but, while always pouring out and sharing these virtues with all men, he remains in the same state of perfection."[5]

As vice, sloth is a failure of love—an aversion to being, a sadness at the good, and an inability to act well. Sloth is not overcome by non-sloth but by the fullness of virtue, by approving or affirming the world, seeing it as God sees it. Given the slackness and sentimentality of our time, notions such as approval and self-affirmation have become wearisome, even distasteful: certainly ill-fitted for the Pauline and Augustinian realism of Catholic Christianity. Still, however mushy the contemporary understandings of affirmation, we are called to passionately love the world, approving of the goodness, glory, and weight it holds, just as God knows and approves. In affirming, we are not offering easy consolation to our wounded esteem, but seeing and willing the truth of being. Approval is not sentiment but an act of intelligence and will; it is fully human (and divine) and not mere emoting.

Since our seeing and willing are damaged by sloth, we require instruction in order to appropriate the fullness of virtue. As God gave two forms of instruction to assist Adam in understanding and welcoming his own subjectivity—the search for a helper and the creation mandates—so we find God's help for our slothful and bored culture. First, as Adam was to welcome Eve in delight, we recover a healthy approval through the practice of Sabbath, which is not an absence or negation of work but a full presence of festive delight in goodness. Sabbath retrains sight and love, guiding us in entering fullness after the bondage of Egypt (sloth, boredom, and nihilism).

If Sabbath retrains us so that we may, like Adam, respond with a delighted "At last," so also the "second" set of God's instructions: the mandates of filling, tending, governing, and keeping the garden.

---

5. St John Chrysostom, *Homilies on St John*, 14, 1 in *The Navarre Bible: The Gospel of St John* (Dublin: Four Courts Press, 1992), 50.

Just as Sabbath resists sloth with a practice of love's approval, sloth needs to be resisted with the fullness of the mandates, a retraining in good work. Sabbath teaches us to be like Adam in loving goodness. But how do we gain capacity in keeping the mandates?

Reaching out to Greatness

In its hatred and sadness, sloth despises our purpose, often revealing itself as a kind of perverted humility refusing the greatness demanded of the human person. Sloth lacks magnanimity, the "aspiration of the spirit to great things, '*extensio animi ad magna*,'" and is far too comfortable settling for less.[6] Firmly confident of the possibilities of our ennobled and redeemed human nature, the magnanimous person "decides in favor of what is, at any given moment, the greater possibility of the human potentiality for being."[7]

Seeking the greater possibility of being at any given moment requires prudence. On the one hand, we know the greatest possibility is communion with God, so distasteful to sloth, but the magnanimous person seeks the good available here and now. Aquinas notes this as well, distinguishing between the proportionate and absolute aspects of magnanimity:

> Now an act may be called great in two ways: in one way proportionately, in another absolutely. An act may be called great proportionately, even if it consists in the use of some small or ordinary thing, if, for instance, one makes a very good use of it: but an act is simply and absolutely great when it consists in the best use of the greatest thing.[8]

Since magnanimity is about great honor, a person is magnanimous "in respect of things that are great absolutely and simply" rather than with respect to the "proportionate" greatness of small or ordinary things.[9] So it is, and yet magnanimity seeks the greatest human

---

6. Pieper, *Faith, Hope, Love*, 101; cf. Kathleen Norris, *Acedia & Me: A Marriage, Monks, and a Writer's Life* (New York: Riverhead Books, 2008), 113.

7. Ibid.

8. Aquinas, *ST* II–II. 129. 1.

9. Ibid.

potentiality for being at any given moment, and most given moments involve small and ordinary things.

Recognizing the magnanimity of the everyday matters especially to the slothful, for whom goodness, great or ordinary, is loathsome. For them, retraining love to will great things in an absolute way may seem an impossible task, so how are they to suddenly welcome friendship with God, with all the weight required for such a task, if even the small weight of proportionate greatness is onerous and taxing? It is no accident that advice given to monastics afflicted with *acedia* is perseverance at their given task, *hypomonè*, staying yoked in one's cell: "the old man, recognizing the suggestions of the demons, said to him, 'Go, eat, drink, sleep, do no work, only do not leave your cell.' For he knew that steadfastness in the cell keeps a monk in the right way."[10] Given the importance of prayer to the monk, the advice remarkably allows a cessation of prayer, hinging the entire struggle on remaining in the cell, even if not praying. As another father put it, "Don't pray at all, just stay in the cell," knowing "what courage, what heroic endurance was needed" when sloth hated, above all, staying "in one place."[11] Cassian recounts the wisdom of Abba Paul who "when his cave was filled with a whole year's work, he would burn up what he had carefully toiled over," needing manual labor to keep him "in one spot . . . persevering in his cell."[12]

The slothful, as Evagrius reminds us, often wish to be elsewhere, suffering an aversion to place, convinced that God could be worshipped best if the monk abandoned his current task. Consequently, the slothful monk, "a runaway, a deserter" often concocts big plans for charity and service, something noble and great,[13] refusing to "see the grace in barren places."[14] Magnanimity, for them, requires first a proportionate greatness in seeing the grace and weightiness of ordinary things.

10. Quoted in Deseille, "Acedia According to the Monastic Tradition," 300; cf. Nault "Acedia," 239.

11. In Norris, *Acedia & Me*, 39.

12. Cassian, *Institutes*, 233.

13. Deseille, "Acedia According to the Monastic Tradition," 298.

14. Kathleen Norris, "Plain old sloth," *Christian Century* (January 11, 2003): 9.

Magnanimity in the Ordinary

For most of us, the cell is our work, whatever happens to be the usual labor of every day. At first, this appears a lack of magnanimity, for the perfection of this particular virtue "is not perceived in every operation . . . but in such operations as are great or difficult: for every power, however imperfect, can extend to ordinary and trifling operations."[15] Prompted by such language, we imagine victories on the battle or playing fields, the soaring oratory of the statesman, or the works of mercy by a renowned saint. Now, such great actions do occur, obviously, with noble women and men exerting incredible will to bring them about. But even those great actions result as the accumulated outcome of many smaller actions, the details of provisioning troops, digging latrines, editing speeches, and bathing the wounds of lepers. Too many of us, too often, fantasize about great deeds, imagining the accolades to follow, only to give up when the toil and strain of the actual work presents itself.

There are reasons to reconsider. Yes, Aquinas says that magnanimity is not about ordinary and trifling operations, for virtue is about "the difficult and the good," and the virtue of magnanimity about the difficult and good of "great honors."[16] But ordinary work, good work, is about the difficult and good; work is given to us by God, and staying put in the cell is hard. The ordinary is extraordinary.

Small things are not trifles. No thing, recall, is ever just itself, but always a creature, bearing in its depths the very agency of God who loves it into existence. Things bear *kâbôd*, for Christ plays in them (even in oranges and onions). Nor is the great weight of things a metaphysical abstraction, for God doesn't "hang out" in things in some static, dead way, but seeks always to communicate himself through them:

> God's purpose or intention of inviting each person into the relational life of the Trinity is not episodic, occurring periodically in each person's life. God is always acting to bring about this inten-

15. Aquinas, *ST* II–II. 129. 2.
16. Ibid.

tion ... at every moment of our existence God is communicating to us who God is, is trying to draw us into an awareness, a consciousness of the reality of who we are in God's sight.[17]

Things are not trifles, although we often have trifling concerns about them, attending to them inordinately. But in themselves, they are not insignificant. Nothing is trifling merely because it is small.

Further, since our full flourishing is supernatural, the "great honors" of social and political life, which we often imagine when thinking of magnanimity, are only relative. Good, perhaps even great, but not ultimate. Magnanimity reaches for the divine good—friendship with God—and keeping this ultimate good in mind preserves the value of natural goods (including honors, ambitions and so on) while insisting on their lack of ultimacy:

> Man is called to a fullness of life which far exceeds the dimensions of his earthly existence, because it consists in sharing the very life of God. The loftiness of this supernatural vocation reveals the greatness and the inestimable value of human life even in its temporal phase. Life in time, in fact, is the fundamental condition, the initial stage and an integral part of the entire unified process of human existence.... At the same time, it is precisely this supernatural calling which highlights the relative character of each individual's earthly life. After all, life on earth is not an "ultimate" but a "penultimate" reality; even so, it remains a sacred reality entrusted to us, to be preserved with a sense of responsibility and brought to perfection in love and in the gift of ourselves to God and to our brothers and sisters.[18]

We know that our ultimate vocation is supernatural rather than natural, rendering our natural vocation "penultimate" but still good. Two errors tempt us: the first lowers our vision and considers natural goods ultimate, while the second wishes to cast off this mortal coil as nothing more than a distraction, maybe even evil, turning only to the supernatural good. Both overlook the integration of supernatural and natural vocations.

17. William A. Barry, *Finding God in All Things: A Companion to the Spiritual Exercises of St. Ignatius* (Notre Dame: Ave Maria Press, 1991), 14.
18. John Paul II, *Evangelium Vitae*, sec. 2.

One of the most beautiful teachings of the Catholic faith is that grace "does not annihilate but presupposes and perfects human nature."[19] Sin does not destroy human nature, and certainly sin does not become our nature, even as nature is deeply wounded, so grace need not lead us out of our nature as something to be escaped. We are redeemed, perfected, and elevated as humans, as evidenced by the Incarnation in which God assumes humanity in order to redeem it. At the same time, grace does more than restore nature to its first Edenic state, for while the grace present in Eden (original rectitude) was a great good, it was not the supernatural fulfillment of communion with God (the light of glory).[20] Grace, without undoing nature and its good, elevates the human beyond our natural end; of all creatures, we are the only ones whose fulfillment includes but goes beyond our nature. Grace presupposes nature, in the sense that humans are graced as humans and not as angels or something else. Grace perfects nature, in that we become fully in act. Grace elevates nature, providing a good disproportionate to our merely natural capacity: "All the faculties of the human being are purified, transformed and uplifted by divine Grace."[21]

Moreover, the natural and supernatural vocations are not disintegrated, as if we have our natural end separated and sealed-off from the supernatural, living our temporal existence until death takes us to a new identity. Not so, for, as *Evangelium Vitae* reminded us, our natural and temporal action is an "integral part of the entire unified process of human existence." Our natural vocation is established in its value and dignity precisely because not ultimate, because dependent on and oriented to the Divine Communion; our nature is a "sacred reality" in that grace presupposes it even while going beyond.

Our natural vocation, given to each of us, is not unrelated to our whole existence. Created by God with the universal vocation to

---

19. Benedict XVI, "General Audience," 16 June 2010, http://www.vatican.va/holy_father/benedict_xvi/audiences/2010/documents/hf_ben-xvi_aud_20100616_e n.html; cf. Aquinas, *ST* I. 1. 8, ad 2.

20. *Catechism of the Catholic Church*, 415, 1028; cf. Aquinas, *ST* I. 94. 1; I. 95. 1.

21. Benedict XVI, "General Audience."

work, keep, fill, and govern the garden, each of us, as human, has this vocation, and thus each of us is called to the personal good of this work. Recalling that the primary end of work is its subjective dimension, or the development and good of the human person, the universal mandates reveal that each person is called to her subjectivity through the task of good work, with the particular vocation of each (farmer, teacher, banker, homemaker), the living out of the universal creation mandates in a way allowing for the irreducible singularity of each person while simultaneously allowing for the differentiation of vocations needed for society and the common good.

In living out our particular tasks, we live out the universal and natural vocation of all humans. Further, since our natural and supernatural vocations are distinct (but not isolated) from each other, since both are concerned with our real and integrated personal good, exercising the ordinary actions of our vocation is the magnanimity of reaching for the "great thing" of our supernatural vocation. Christian life cannot be understood as anything other than a "permanent and daily response to a call . . . not heard only at one particular moment in time but . . . progressively drawn out as the believer becomes more like Christ."[22] Called by God at creation to a vocation, the "Christological form of the vocation implies a call to more and more adopt a filial profile in Christ."[23] Becoming sons of God through Christ, grace perfects us, but this grace is given to us as we live and work now, and our vocation is the place of our "living and creative" integration of "our actions and the unification of the person."[24] Redemption is concrete, and God creates and heals in history, including our personal histories as we live them out in our ordinary days. God works in us, through grace, so that as we cooperate in our redemption through everyday work, the primary purpose of which is our completion, we become his friends, stretching out to reach for that divine and supernatural good. We are mag-

---

22. Livio Melina, *The Epiphany of Love: Toward a Theological Understanding of Christian Action* (Grand Rapids: Eerdmans, 2010), 95.
23. Ibid., 96.
24. Ibid., 97.

nanimous, reaching out to ultimacy, insofar as we reach out to the mundane through good work.

Very Human Virtues

Sloth's cure is staying in the cell, remaining yoked to the work God has given, including the universal vocation of the creation mandates, the task of our particular vocations as individuals, and the various disciplines of a life well-ordered. We stay in the cell in very concrete ways—keeping the prayers, finishing the report, paying our bills on time, wiping away childish tears, doing the dishes, cleaning the car, caring for our tools—through staying in the quotidian, the mundane ordinary work.[25] While perhaps unromantic, this settling into our cell allows for virtue, since natural virtue requires habituation. Mere repetition may not make us virtuous, but there is no virtue without repetition, and so we stay put, sink our roots deep, and find the rich soil of virtue. In part this is because virtue, as a firm characteristic, demands a training of taste, including developing a discriminating palate through experiencing good things which we may initially find off-putting and distasteful. So we try again, in time refining our dispositions until we take pleasure in fine and beautiful things.

Parents can confirm this, remembering the contest of convincing their child that *spaghetti alla carbonara* (or whatever delicacy was planned) really was better than chicken fingers and strawberry flavored milk. Also, and more intimately, as they recall their own transformation from chic concert-goer to exhausted parent and chicken finger chef, to someone who rediscovered playfulness and learned to delight in the squeals and squawks of a happy toddler. Exhausting? Sometimes, but a new character forms with every nap, meal, diaper, meltdown, wet bed, and smile. We become the people we are by what we choose to do again.

---

25. While the work is adapted in part from *Acedia & Me*, the title of another work by Kathleen Norris is revelatory, *The Quotidian Mysteries: Laundry, Liturgy and "Women's Work"* (Mahwah: Paulist, 1998). For another helpful recovery of the grace of the everyday, see Margaret Kim Peterson, *Keeping House: The Litany of Everyday Life* (San Francisco: Jossey-Bass, 2007).

Small is Beautiful

Our own time seems to imagine that friendship with God is a matter of enthusiasm and emotions, as if God is worshipped only when someone feels like they have worshipped. Those feelings can be nice, of course, even an encouragement and spur to stay in the cell for another day, but genuinely human reaching out to God is a matter of will, involving all the disciplines and mastery required for governing ourselves. As the desert elders reminded their disciples, eat or drink or rest, pray or not, just so long as you stay in your cell. One needn't feel all that much about it, just persevere, keep the yoke, and bear the weightiness of responsibility.

Too often, spirituality is imagined as something recondite or exciting: mystical or exotic. Indeed, it can and does include these, but for most of us, most of the time, genuine spirituality is a matter of reaching out for God (and finding him) in the busy materiality of our work. As in the Incarnation and the Eucharist, God gives himself through matter, and the spiritual life is not unweighted by material things:

> The redemption wrought by Christ and entrusted to the saving mission of the Church is certainly of the supernatural order. This dimension is not a delimitation of salvation but rather an integral expression of it. The supernatural is not to be understood as an entity or a place that begins where the natural ends, but as the raising of the natural to a higher plane. In this way nothing of the created or the human order is foreign to or excluded from the supernatural or theological order of faith and grace, rather it is found within it, taken on and elevated by it.[26]

A genuinely spiritual or supernatural life is materialized in our work of culture making, and it makes both us and the world more human, more perfected in our subjectivity. As we are sanctified, so our work is sanctified, throughout the whole range of human endeavor: "[the Church] is attentive to . . . the authentically human and humanizing aspects—of social life. Society—and with it, politics, the economy, labour, law, culture—is not simply a secular and

---

26. *Compendium of the Social Doctrine of the Church*, 64.

worldly reality, and therefore outside or foreign to the message and economy of salvation."[27]

Since grace perfects nature, everything genuinely human is welcomed and elevated by the supernatural, and nothing good is unfit for divine approval. At the same time, grace presupposes nature and so the more genuinely human we are, the more grace has to perfect. The integrative relationship between grace and nature is comprehensive, and it is usually the case that grace perfects best what is already developed in keeping with its natural ends. If we are lazy in our studies, for instance, it is unlikely that all our prayers for knowledge will effect much, even as the diligent student, perfected by the grace of charity, bears much fruit. The finely tended and pruned roots of nature planted in well-cultivated soul flourish into grace-filled splendor, but a nature harshly treated or stunted in rocky soil often bears few or small fruits, even with divine assistance (Matt 13:1–9, Sower and the Seed). Grace transforms, yes, but normally grace develops the person in concert with their human virtues: "How is . . . fortitude to be sown in a Christian who will not struggle against small habits of laziness or comfort seeking. . . ?"[28] It is in good soil that human virtues take root, providing the material for grace to elevate, but the good Christian must be the good human first.[29]

To attain the great honors of magnanimity, begin with ordinary human virtues acquired through everyday human work done well. Here the small details are everything. Normal work demands patience, carefulness, craftsmanship, knowledge, fortitude, moderation, sociality, prudence, judgment, restraint, taste, honesty, and more, each developed and acquired through other occasions of repetition and action. To act well in any matter, great or small, demands a mature and stable character forged through many other instances of patience, fortitude, moderation, and so on; to act well even in some small matter requires great, difficult, and sustained operations

27. Ibid., 62.
28. Francis Fernandez-Carvajal, *In Conversation with God*, vol. 4 (London: Scepter, 2010), 204.
29. Ibid., 205.

of virtue, and so any work done well is magnanimous, especially if done with an eye to our supernatural vocation.

Our Ordinary Lord

Work is given by divine command to fill, tend, keep, and govern the world, and it is the means by which we sustain our lives and society even as developing our own subjectivity and cooperating with God's grace in our perfection.[30] So it should not surprise us that the Apostle Paul labored at tent-making, or that Joseph was a craftsman, or that the Virgin gave her fiat to all the usual tasks and labors of her time and responsibilities. Nor were these tasks merely incidental to their supernatural work, as if they had time to fill until the main event, or as if the worldly demands of making a living and keeping a roof over one's head were necessary evils suffered while turning as often as possible to the "real things" whenever a spare moment presented itself. Not so. We meet God in our work, we reach out to his divine friendship when we stay in our cell, loving our place and the goodness residing in its things and tasks and mandates. We are perfected, our objective world is developed, our character is sanctified, the fully integrated Gospel is born witness, and we co-redeem the garden through our work, even as we provide the adornments with which God, in delight and pride, fills his eternal and cosmic temple. Good work is what we are for, and through it, assisted by grace, all manner of things are made well.

Nor is the value of work confirmed merely by Paul and Joseph and Mary, for the entirety of the Holy Family ply their trade, with Jesus joining in. Having begun his ministry, he is rejected in his hometown, as merely the carpenter (Mk 6:3). His neighbors had known him and his family, and they observed nothing unusual; our Lord ate and drank as others, dressed as they did, slept, learned, stumbled, wept, grew weary, had friends, obeyed his mother, and worked. Even those who knew him well, those familiar with him for his entire life, identify him by his trade, as the son of a carpenter

---

30. Ibid., 474.

and a carpenter himself. Jesus labors and works, and does so for the vast majority of his life, for thirty years.

While Scripture tells us little prior to his public ministry, we would be mistaken to conclude that the hours in the workshop are irrelevant to our salvation. We are redeemed not only by Christ's death, not only by his resurrection, but also, as the Litany of the Saints reminds us, by his Incarnation, birth, baptism, fasting, passion, and ascension. That is, our redemption comes by his whole life, the vast majority of which is spent at ordinary work effecting salvation for us and the whole world. All of creation is redeemed in Christ, a God who labors with tools and matter, and all of creation is perfected and elevated as God in Christ shapes and sands. Those bits of wood and the tools which worked them, held in the hands of God himself, were no trifles, however ordinary; for us, created in his image, called to work, these very same things bear his infinite glorious weight deep down, and as we reach for them we grasp him.

A Good Night's Work

Staying in the cell vanquishes sloth since remaining under the yoke of the good work given to us by God satisfies our universal and particular vocations and reaches out magnanimously for the divine good of God's friendship. If we remain at our work we love the world back into graciousness as we refuse sloth's abhorrence of place, sadness at the good, and refusal to act. When we act, we operate in keeping with the richness of the world and our own selves, and so encounter God as our friend.

While the work may be Sabbath-like as it recognizes and delights in the goodness of things and the labor which keeps them, the work drains and spends us. How easy to rest from our proper labor for just a little bit, looking outside the cell, imagining another, better place, wishing for escape, for weightless freedom. Often, just at that tempting moment, when we long to leave the cell, our Lord asks us to stay put, to do as he has called.

At one point, Jesus climbs into Peter's boat and tells him to "Put out into the deep and let down your nets for a catch," even though, as Peter reminds Jesus, they had "toiled all night and took nothing"

(Lk 5:4–5). He obeys because Jesus asked, landing such a catch that the nets break and multiple boats sink under the load. At the word of Christ, Peter sets out into the deep, again, after a futile night of toil in which he exercised all the worldly knowledge gained from years of practicing his work. But he is asked, so he stays to his work, and by grace, perfecting his labor, bears much fruit.

The slothful would have gone home—tired, disappointed, angry, spiteful, wishing for new work in a better place. Peter stays at it, and from his ordinary work, the rock of the Church is perfected and he becomes a fisher of men, with the salvation of the entire world resting in his nets.

Conclusion

A Cold Response to Life

In John Williams's *Butcher's Crossing*, set in the Kansas prairies of the 1870s, a young Will Andrews flees Harvard and his father's Unitarianism for the open freedom of the plains: "Sometimes after listening to the droning voices in the chapel and in the classrooms, he had fled the confines . . . to the fields and woods. . . . There in some small solitude . . . uplifted into infinite space; the meanness and the constriction he had felt were dissipated in the wildness about him."[1] Chafing at the limits of society, he longs for "wildness . . . a freedom and a goodness, a hope and a vigor that he perceived to underlie all the familiar things of his life." (21)

Upon reaching the town of Butcher's Crossing, he hires Miller, a famed buffalo hunter claiming to know of a massive herd in a hidden valley in Colorado. Even with winter approaching, Will agrees, and they set out, confident they will return before the snows, rich in hides and wild vitality. To his delight, "he was leaving the city more and more, withdrawing into the wilderness," (48–49) entering a purer, more beautiful nature with its "quality of absoluteness . . . whose limits and extents were undefined." (41–42)

Unused to hard riding, Will finds the first day brutal, a searing pain of muscles and headache turning into a kind of numbness on subsequent days. He "found himself less and less conscious of any movement," forgetting even selfhood as he "felt himself to be like the land, without identity or shape." (77–78) Miller, the boss of the party, becomes animalistic, "one with his horse," sitting in his saddle "as if he were a natural extension," speaking infrequently, merely "sniff-[ing] at the land" as they search for water. (77–78)

---

1. John Williams, *Butcher's Crossing* (New York: New York Review of Books, 1988), 45–46. As this work is cited often in this chapter, hereafter page references will be given in parentheses following the quotation.

Despite the odds, they find buffalo, thousands of the beasts, and Miller begins the merciless slaughter. The great trick, we learn, is to "buffalo" the herd, dispatching the leader and throwing the rest into confusion so they loop back into the kill zone. Miller fires until his rifle glows red, changes guns and continues, leaving corpses for the crew to skin. Will is surprised to find the bison's "wild dignity" destroyed. (130) All that remains is the murderous "dance, a thunderous minuet created by the wildness" of the men. (135) During the first big kill of 155 bison, he "came to see Miller as a mechanism, an automaton ... and he came to see Miller's destruction of the buffalo, not as a lust for blood ... or hides ... he came to see the destruction as a cold, *mindless response to ... life.*" (135, emphasis added) Confronted directly with the task of skinning and butchering, Will is distraught, he "sliced blindly, awkwardly... the rotten smell of the buffalo's half-digested food billowed out. He held his breath and hacked more desperately" before its entrails spill onto him, causing him to vomit and flee. (145)

But Miller won't leave, even though winter threatens and they have many more hides than they can transport. Rather than acting prudently, Miller won't even speak, becoming "totally intent upon his kill," communicating with "curt motions ... and growlings deep in his throat." (155, 159) He stops bathing and the black powder collects on his face like "a permanent part of his skin." (159)

Then the first flakes; the bison go mad and the men fearful. Trapped, they are snowed in, spending the first blizzard in rancid hides described like wombs from which they emerge on the third day as new men into a sea of white, snowed in. They have returned to wildness, absolutely free. And it means death.

John Paul II warns that freedom without truth propped up the culture of death. Seeking to escape constraints, some seek wildness, congratulating themselves on their authenticity while granting "boundless space" to a "destructive and irresponsible freedom."[2] Promised infinite space, but finding spiritual exhaustion: "already a

---

2. Aleksandr Solzhenitsyn, *The Solzhenitsyn Reader: New and Essential Writings, 1947–2005*, ed. Edward E. Ericson, Jr. and Daniel J. Mahoney (Wilmington: ISI Books, 2009), 566.

universal spiritual demise is upon us; a physical one is about to flare up and engulf us and our children, while we continue to smile sheepishly and babble."[3] Looking to find a new dignity in wildness, but instead, like Miller, gaining a cold, mindless hatred of life.

Like all the demonic thoughts, the vice of sloth promises life but brings death; the way of the Cross demands death but gives life. Given our deep *acedia*, we choose the lie, recoiling in abject disgust and sadness at the truth of being. Thinking we retain vitality by rejecting the Cross, we stumble into enervation, unable to act, impotent. Glancing at our own society, we observe remarkable dynamism in trade, technology, transportation, entertainment—really incredible advances—but find inertia and tiredness in the domain of value. We seem to have no will for life, choosing sterile sex, rejecting (or deforming) marriage, dismembering nascent life in the womb, while endlessly seeking pleasant distractions—anything to keep us from facing honestly the truth of our being and its noble demands. Compared to the youthful effervescence of the saints, desire's empire seems like a love of death, alternating between crazed attempts to prolong the baubles of our entertainments, whatever the expense or exploitation, or wearily sinking into despair, refusing to propagate our culture or bodies. We know not what we are for, or if we do we shrink from its weighty labor.

The world exists because God is the fullness of self-communicative love, and this effusiveness governs and exists at the heart of all creation, which is very good. God delights in it all—"rose-moles all in stipple upon trout that swim; Fresh-firecoal chestnut falls; finches' wings"—approving its profound goodness, the deep weight of existence it carries.[4] He loves the world so much as to elevate creation in the person of Adam, raising the dirt into a being granted the God-like responsibility of filling the garden, even allowing Adam to cooperate with his supernatural vocation through the grace of work. We, like God, have been tasked to approve of the world, perfecting ourselves and it through our festive work.

Instead, the slothful hate the noble task God has given, wishing

---

3. Ibid., 556.
4. Hopkins, "Pied Beauty."

A Cold Response to Life

only for indolent lightness. In bored sloth our loves grow cold, and we see nothing to cause delight, wantonly destroying ourselves and the good world in a pique of sadness. Many are tired now, their love affair with life diminished, spent by clawing efforts to remain weightless. Hatred, sadness, impotence—a terrible covenant. Sloth, like Judge Holden, wraps them in its horrible embrace, and they sink into death rather than reaching out for life.

Still, for all that, there remains the dearest freshness deep down things; if only we love.

Bibliography

Aquinas, Thomas. *On Evil*. Translated by Jean Oesterle. Notre Dame: University of Notre Dame Press, 1995.

———. *Summa Contra Gentiles*. Translated by Vernon Bourke. Notre Dame: University of Notre Dame Press, 1975.

———. *Summa Theologica*. Translated by the Fathers of the English Dominican Province. Notre Dame: Christian Classics, 1981.

Augustine. *Confessions*. Translated by Henry Chadwick. New York: Oxford University Press, 1991.

———. *The Trinity*. Translated by Edmund Hill. Brooklyn: New City Press, 1991.

Barry, William A. *Finding God in All Things: A Companion to the Spiritual Exercises of St. Ignatius*. Notre Dame: Ave Maria Press, 1991.

Belloc, Hilaire. "The Catholic Sun." Poemhunter.com. http://www.poemhunter.com/poem/the-catholic-sun-2/.

Benedict XVI, "General Audience." Vatican, 16 June 2010. http://www.vatican.va/holy_father/benedict_xvi/audiences/2010/documents/hf_ben-xvi_aud_20100616_en.html.

Bernard of Clairvaux. *Commentary on the Song of Songs*. Etext arranged by Darrell Wright. Internet Archive, 2008. https://archive.org/details/St.BernardOnTheSongOfSongs.

Berry, Wendell. *The Art of the Commonplace: The Agrarian Essays of Wendell Berry*. Edited by Norman Wirzba. Washington, DC: Shoemaker & Hoard, 2002.

Capon, Robert Farrar. *The Supper of the Lamb: A Culinary Reflection*. New York: Macmillan, 1969.

Cassian, John. *The Conferences*. Translated by Boniface Ramsey. Vol. 57 of *Ancient Christian Writers*, edited by Walter Burghardt, John Dillon, and Dennis D. McManus. New York: Paulist Press, 1997.

———. *The Institutes*. Translated by Boniface Ramsey. Vol. 58 of *Ancient Christian Writers*, edited by Dennis D. McManus. New York: Newman Press, 2000.

Catechism of the Catholic Church, 2nd edition. Washington, DC: United States Catholic Conference, 1997.

Chesterton, G.K. *Saint Thomas Aquinas.* New York: Image Books, 1956.

Clarke, W. Norris. *Person and Being, The Aquinas Lecture, 1993.* Milwaukee: Marquette University Press, 1993.

Crislip, Andrew. "The Sin of Sloth or the Illness of the Demons? The Demon of Acedia in Early Christian Monasticism," *Harvard Theological Review* 98:2 (2005): 146–153.

Crouch, Andy. *Culture Making: Recovering our Creative Calling.* Downers Grove: IVP Books, 2008.

Deseille, Placide. "Acedia According to the Monastic Tradition," *Cisterian Studies Quarterly* 37:3 (2002): 297–301.

Duffy, Eamon. *The Stripping of the Altars: Traditional Religion in England c. 1400–1580.* New Haven: Yale University Press, 1992.

Eco, Umberto. *Art and Beauty in the Middle Ages.* Translated by Hugh Bredin. New Haven: Yale University Press, 1986.

Eliot, T.S. *The Waste Land and Other Poems.* San Diego: Harvest, 1962.

Fernandez-Carvajal, Francis. *In Conversation with God.* Vol. 4. London: Scepter, 2010.

Fisher, M.F.K. *The Art of Eating.* Hoboken: Wiley Publishing, 2004.

Gilson, Etienne. *The Spirit of Medieval Philosophy.* Translated by A.H.C. Downes. Notre Dame: University of Notre Dame Press, 1991.

Goodstein, Elizabeth S. *Experience Without Qualities: Boredom and Modernity.* Stanford: Stanford University Press, 2005.

Grant, George. *English-Speaking Justice.* Toronto: Anansi, 1985.

———. "Faith and the Multiversity." *Communio* 40 (Spring 2013): 161–196.

Gregory the Great. *Pastoral Care.* Translated by Henry Davis. Vol. 11 of *Ancient Christian Writers,* ed. Johannes Quasten and Joseph C. Plumpe. New York: Newman Press, 1950.

Guardini, Romano. *Letters from Lake Como: Explorations in Technology and the Human Race.* Translated by Geoffrey W. Bromiley. Grand Rapids: Eerdmans, 1994.

Hanby, Michael. "The Culture of Death, the Ontology of Boredom, and the Resistance of Joy," *Communio* 31 (2004): 181–99.

Hegeman, David Bruce. *Plowing in Hope: Toward a Biblical Theology of Culture.* Moscow, ID: Canon Press, 2007.

Heidegger, Martin. *Basic Writings*. Edited by David Farrell Krell. New York: Harper SanFrancisco, 1993.

Heschel, Abraham Joshua. *The Sabbath: Its Meaning for Modern Man*. New York: Farrar, Straus and Giroux, 1951.

Hopkins, Gerard Manley. *The Major Works*. Edited by Catherine Phillips. New York: Oxford University Press, 2009.

John Paul II. *Evangelium Vitae. Encyclical Letter The Gospel of Life*. Boston: Pauline Books, 1995.

———. *Laborem Exercens. Encyclical Letter On Human Work*. Vatican, 1981. http://www.vatican.va/holy_father/john_paul_ii/encyclicals/documents/hf_jp-ii_enc_14091981_laborem-exercens_en.html.

———. *Man and Woman He Created Them: A Theology of the Body*. Translated by Michael Waldstein. Boston: Pauline Books, 2006.

———. *Redemptor Hominis. Encyclical Letter The Redeemer of Man*. Boston: Pauline Books, 1979.

———. *Veritatis Splendor. Encyclical Letter The Splendor of Truth*. Boston: Pauline Books, 1993.

Julian of Norwich. *Revelations of Divine Love*. Translated by Clifton Wolters. New York: Penguin Books, 1966.

Kant, Immanuel. *Critique of Pure Reason*. Translated by Werner S. Pluhar. Indianapolis: Hackett, 1996.

Kass, Leon R. *The Beginning of Wisdom: Reading Genesis*. Chicago: University of Chicago Press, 2006.

———. "The Ten Commandments: Why the Decalogue Matters." *Mosaic Magazine*, June 2013. http://mosaicmagazine.com/essay/2013/06/the-ten-commandments/.

Konyndyk DeYoung, Rebecca. "Resistance to the Demands of Love: Aquinas on the Vice of *Acedia*," *The Thomist* 68 (2004): 173–204.

Kuhn, Reinhard. *The Demon of Noontide: Ennui in Western Literature*. Princeton: Princeton University Press, 1976.

Kundera, Milan. *The Unbearable Lightness of Being*. New York: Harper Perennial, 1991.

Kuyper, Abraham. *Lectures on Calvinism*. Grand Rapids: Eerdmans, 1931.

Lichtenstein, Aharon. "To Cultivate and to Guard: The Universal Duties of Mankind." Adapted by Reuven Ziegler. *The Israel Koschitzky Virtual Beit Midrash*, Winter 1986–87. http://vbm-torah.org/archive/develop/01develop.htm.

Bibliography

Lonergan, Bernard. *Collected Works of Bernard Lonergan*. Edited by Frederick E. Crowe and Robert M. Doran. Vol. 3, *Insight: A Study of Human Understanding*. Toronto: University of Toronto, 1992.
———. *Method in Theology*. New York: Seabury Press, 1972.

MacIntyre, Alasdair. *After Virtue: A Study in Moral Theory*. Notre Dame: University of Notre Dame Press, 1984.

Maritain, Jacques. *The Person and the Common Good*. Translated by John J. Fitzgerald. Notre Dame: University of Notre Dame Press, 1966.

Maturin, B. W. *Self-Knowledge and Self-Discipline*. London: Longmans, Green, and Co., 1909. Reprinted by Forgotten Books, 2012.

McCarthy, Cormac. *Blood Meridian, or The Evening Redness in the West*. New York: Vintage International, 1992.

Melchin, Kenneth R. *History, Ethics, and Emergent Probability: Ethics, Society and History in the work of Bernard Lonergan*, 2nd edition. The Lonergan Website, 1999.

Melina, Livio. *The Epiphany of Love: Toward a Theological Understanding of Christian Action*. Grand Rapids: Eerdmans, 2010.

Mouw, Richard J. *When the Kings Come Marching In: Isaiah and the New Jerusalem*, Revised Edition. Grand Rapids: Eerdmans, 2002.

Nault, Jean-Charles. "Acedia: Enemy of Spiritual Joy," *Communio* 31 (Summer 2004): 236–58.

The Navarre Bible: The Gospel of St John. Dublin: Four Courts Press, 1992.

The New Oxford Annotated Bible. New York. Oxford University Press, 1977.

Norris, Kathleen. *Acedia & Me: A Marriage, Monks, and a Writer's Life*. New York: Riverhead Books, 2008.

———. "Plain old sloth," *Christian Century* (January 11, 2003): 8–9.

———. *The Quotidian Mysteries: Laundry, Liturgy and "Women's Work."* Mahwah: Paulist, 1998.

Percy, Walker. *Lost in the Cosmos: The Last Self-Help Book*. New York: Picador, 1983.

Peterson, Margaret Kim. *Keeping House: The Litany of Everyday Life*. San Francisco: Jossey-Bass, 2007.

Pieper, Joseph. *Faith, Hope, Love*. San Francisco: Ignatius, 1991.

———. *In Tune with the World: A Theory of Festivity*. Translated by Richard and Clara Winston. South Bend: St. Augustine's Press, 1999.

———. *Leisure the Basis of Culture.* Translated by Alexander Dru. New York: Mentor-Omega Books, 1963.

———. *Only the Lover Sings: Art and Contemplation.* Translated by Lothar Krauth. San Francisco: Ignatius Press, 1990.

Plantinga, Cornelius. *Engaging God's World: A Christian Vision of Faith, Learning, and Living.* Grand Rapids: Eerdmans, 2002.

Pollan, Michael. *The Omnivore's Dilemma: A Natural History of Four Meals.* New York: Penguin Books, 2006.

Pontifical Council for Justice and Peace, *Compendium of the Social Doctrine of the Church.* Washington, DC: USCCB Publishing, 2004.

Ratzinger, Joseph. *'In the Beginning…' A Catholic Understanding of the Story of Creation and the Fall.* Translated by Boniface Ramsey. Grand Rapids: Eerdmans, 1995.

Reno, R. R. "Empire of Desire." *First Things* (June/July 2014): 25–30.

Rhonheimer, Martin. *Changing the World: The Timeliness of Opus Dei.* New York: Scepter, 2009.

Sacks, Jonathan. *To Heal a Fractured World: The Ethics of Responsibility.* New York: Schocken Books, 2005.

Schmitz, Kenneth. *Recovery of Wonder.* Montreal & Kingston: McGill-Queen's University Press, 2005.

Schuessler Jennifer. "Our Boredom, Ourselves," *New York Times,* January 21, 2010. http://www.nytimes.com/2010/01/24/books/review/Schuessler-t.html.

Second Vatican Ecumenical Council. "Pastoral Constitution on the Church in the Modern World. *Guadium et Spes.*" 1965. http://www.vatican.va/archive/hist_councils/ii_vatican_council/documents/vat-ii_const_19651207_gaudium-et-spes_en.html.

Snell, R. J. "The Gift of Good Sex: Thinking Contraception Anew." *The Covenant Quarterly* 66 (Summer 2008): 24–37.

———. "Lust to Annihilate: Terrible Covenant of Sloth." *The City* (Winter 2011): 82–93.

———. *The Perspective of Love: Natural Law in a New Mode.* Eugene: Pickwick Publications, 2014.

———. *Through a Glass Darkly: Bernard Lonergan and Richard Rorty on Knowing without a God's-Eye View.* Milwaukee: Marquette University Press, 2006.

———. "Sloth Transposed: The Friendless Universe." *Lonergan*

Workshop 24 (2013): 407–20.

Soloveitchik, Joseph B. *The Lonely Man of Faith*. New York: Three Leaves Press, 1965.

Solzhenitsyn, Aleksandr. *The Solzhenitsyn Reader: New and Essential Writings, 1947–2005*. Edited by Edward E. Ericson, Jr. and Daniel J. Mahoney. Wilmington: ISI Books, 2009.

Spacks, Patricia Meyer. *Boredom: The Literary History of a State of Mind*. Chicago: University of Chicago Press, 1995.

Svendsen, Lars. *A Philosophy of Boredom*. London: Reaktion Books, 2005.

Taylor, Charles. *The Ethics of Authenticity*. Cambridge: Harvard University Press, 1991.

———. *A Secular Age*. Cambridge: Belknap Press of Harvard University Press, 2007.

———. *Sources of the Self*. Cambridge: Harvard University Press, 1989.

Tischner, Józef. *The Spirit of Solidarity*. Translated by Marek B. Zaleski and Benjamin Fiore. New York: Harper and Row, 1984.

Van Leeuwen, Raymond C. "Cosmos, Temple, House: Building and Wisdom in Mesopotamia and Israel." In *From the Foundations to the Crenellations: Essays on Temple Building in the Ancient Near East and Hebrew Bible*, edited by Mark J. Boda and Jamie Novotny, 399–421. *Alter Orient und Altes Testament*, Band 366. Münster: Ugarit-Verlag, 2010.

Volf, Miroslav. *Work in the Spirit: Toward a Theology of Work*. Eugene: Wipf and Stock, 1991.

Wadell, Paul J. and Darin H. Davis. "Tracking the Toxins of *Acedia*: Reenvisioning Moral Education." In *The Schooled Heart: Moral Formation in American Higher Education*, edited by Michael D. Beaty and Douglas V. Henry. Waco: Baylor University Press, 2007.

Wenzel, Siegfried. *The Sin of Sloth: Acedia in Medieval Thought and Literature*. Chapel Hill: University of North Carolina Press, 1967.

Williams, John. *Butcher's Crossing*. New York: New York Review of Books, 1988.

Williams, Rowan. "Creation." In *Augustine through the Ages: An Encyclopedia*. General editor Allan D. Fitzgerald. Grand Rapids: Eerdmans, 1999.

————. *Grace and Necessity: Reflections on Art and Love*. Harrisburg: Morehouse, 2005.

Wirzba, Norman. *Living the Sabbath: Discovering the Rhythms of Rest and Delight*. Grand Rapids: Brazos, 2006.

Wolters, Albert. *Creation Regained: Biblical Basics for a Reformational Worldview*. Grand Rapids: Eerdmans, 1985.

Wolterstorff, Nicholas. *Art in Action: Toward a Christian Aesthetic*. Grand Rapids: Eerdmans, 1980.

41225239R00084

Made in the USA
Lexington, KY
04 May 2015